NOT BUYING IT

THE ART OF SELLING TO SCIENTISTS, DOCTORS, AND OTHER PROFESSIONAL SKEPTICS

A strategic sales and marketing guide for persuading the world's most skeptical audiences.

Hamid Ghanadan

Not Buying It
The Art of Selling to Scientists, Doctors, and Other Professional Skeptics— A strategic sales and marketing guide for persuading the world's most skeptical audiences.

© 2025 Hamid Ghanadan

This publication is designed to provide accurate and authoritative information regarding the subject matter covered. It is sold with the understanding that the publisher is not engaged in rendering legal, accounting, or other professional services. If you require legal advice or other expert assistance, you should seek the services of a competent professional.

Design and cover art by Peaceful Profits.

Paperback ISBN: 978-1-967587-49-0
Hardcover ISBN: 978-1-967587-51-3
eBook ISBN: 978-1-967587-50-6

DISCLAIMER: The author makes no guarantees to the results you'll achieve by reading this book. All business requires risk and hard work. The results and client case studies presented in this book represent results achieved working directly with LINUS. The information contained in this book is provided for educational purposes only and should not be construed as legal, financial, tax, or investment advice. Readers are strongly encouraged to consult with a qualified and licensed professional who can provide advice tailored to their individual circumstances. Laws, regulations, and financial practices vary across countries, states, and regions. Market conditions, returns, and outcomes will differ over time and cannot be guaranteed. While every effort has been made to provide accurate and timely information at the time of writing, we make no representations or warranties regarding completeness, accuracy, or applicability. We are not making any official legal or financial recommendations. The examples, figures, and principles presented herein are for illustrative and educational purposes only. Any decisions you make are solely your responsibility.

To Marzieh. For everything.

*"If you want to build a ship, don't drum up the men
to gather wood, divide the work, and give orders.
Instead, teach them to yearn for the vast
and endless sea."*

–Antoine de Saint-Exupéry

Contents

Introduction

Corvallis, Oregon, 1995

An anxious cough broke the gentle hum of the ultracentrifuge that was running in the corner of the otherwise silent lab. I looked over, observing the man in a suit, wearing a lapel pin donning a green and white company logo shaped like a pill, a stack of thick product catalogs in his hand.

"Hi! Do you guys work on DNA here?"

I shook my head. "No."

"Proteins?" he quickly followed up, with the slightest note of uncertainty in his voice.

"Nope," I said again.

I could see in his mind that he was scanning his product catalog. Finding nothing, he placed a copy of the green and white catalog on my desk. He backed away with his arms outstretched as if he might get attacked (though at 5'8", or 1.72 meters, I don't cut a particularly threatening figure).

"Look through our catalog, and if there's anything you need, give me a call." He flashed me the kind of smile that drips with defeat, before dashing down the biochemistry department's main hallway and out of view.

Poor guy, I thought, returning to my experiment. *His job is to walk into scientists' labs who supposedly know everything and try to sell them stuff!*

For the rest of the day, the thought never left me. How *do* you sell to such a skeptical audience?

This question, asked in the earliest hours of the digital communications age of the mid-1990s, led me to quit my trajectory as a biochemist, start my career and company, LINUS, and write this book. Weird flex; I know.

Why You're Here

Whether you've spent your career in sales or marketing in life science and healthcare or you're just starting your career in these technical fields, you've likely noticed that scientists, doctors and other professionals make decisions differently than the typical consumer. They ask many technical questions. They crave lots of data. They set up extensive evaluations.

And yet, you get the sense that there's some other force at play.

Think of the many times you deployed a webinar with a key opinion leader presenting amazing science or medical outcomes that featured your product. Hundreds of your target audience registered, attended, and agreed to hear from you about your product.

Yet, little to no actual sales arose from the effort.

Or think about the time when you walked out of a sales meeting with a group of scientific or medical decision-makers, when you were sure you had them. They were engaged, asking all kinds of scientific questions. You successfully answered every question and objection about the science, workflow, economics, and how your offering will "move their research further" or "improve patient outcomes," only to have them ghost your follow-up calls.

There's some other force at play, indeed.

Technical audiences think and make decisions just like every other human, but there are ways in which they also act very differently. The good news is their decision-making follows a very specific and repeatable pattern that you can use to effectively persuade them.

Successful commercialization involves a deep understanding of your consumer's psychology. Humans have evolved over millennia, and though technical professionals dominantly use their prefrontal cortex, many aspects of our brain remain animalistic. In our attempt to navigate the gauntlet of technical details that a scientific or medical buyer demands, we often forget this fact.

If we do take this fact into consideration, however, and study the psychology of technical decision-making, we realize that sales and marketing are about much more than technical communication. Successfully persuading technical professionals such as scientists and doctors requires strategies that go far beyond articulating functional and technical benefits, backed by evidence. It requires counterintuitive thinking.

Every business endeavor is essentially a bet. You bet that a market needs—and is willing to exchange money—to alleviate their need. Your job in product management, market development, marketing, and sales is to stack the odds of that bet in your favor. **You need a secret superpower in the form of a key insight about your audience, that no one else has, to influence the outcome of your bet and not fall victim to the statistical odds of the market.**

The predecessor of this book was first published in 2012 as *Persuading Scientists: Marketing to the World's Most Skeptical Audience.* I've now updated it and broadened the scope in this second writing to include other technical professionals, who are also innately skeptical, such as doctors, engineers, and even the finance community, all of whom play a role in purchasing life science tools, services, diagnostics, medical devices, therapeutics and other health technologies.

While there are countless resources that teach sales and marketing concepts in B2B, B2C, or B2whatever, this book is specifically made for your industry. **The timeless strategies from the first edition remain the same, with updated case studies, research, and stories to help you master sales and marketing, create true demand, and maintain control of your high-stakes conversations with your audience and prospects.**

Why This Book is Relevant

Since the initial publication of the original book, tens of thousands of my readers have enjoyed successful careers and are now leaders in our industry. I've been truly lucky that many of them are now my friends and mentors. They have collectively told me that there's a need to usher in the next generation of leaders. But the world has changed so radically in the 15 years since I wrote the initial book that it feels like malpractice to republish the original text. Hence, this updated version, which has led to a whole new book, in my opinion.

If you're here because of the first edition of this book, thank you. Thank you for trusting me to provide a little bit of insight in your journey toward mastery.

If this is our first time meeting, hello and welcome. I'm here to break down marketing and sales principles with tangible examples that work specifically for your industry. Many of the strategies remain perpetual, even with advancing technology that's changing the landscape, such as artificial intelligence (AI).

Like every tool since the beginning of time, AI makes it easier to do something today that was harder yesterday. The vast majority of initial use cases for the large language models that we short-hand as AI revolve around efficiency gains, which will quickly result in an intolerable cacophony of white noise in your target audience's inboxes, text messages, conferences, and media feeds.

Although AI can produce yesterday's content at a rapid rate and promise more effective targeting, it will quickly erode efficacy. Apply principles of decision-making to AI, though, and you are far more likely to achieve greater results than ever imaginable.

So, while this book comes at a pivotal time, the core message remains the same: exceptional sales and marketing isn't about applying any tool. It's about having an exceptional

strategy. The core ingredient for an effective strategy is a *key insight* about the psychology of your audience. Finding that insight requires having empathy for your target audience.

To keep this text focused on the fundamental principles of this book, I have left out any discussions about specific tactics, tools and technology. Instead, my team and I have created a dedicated community where we provide exclusive content to a closed-door community of insiders on a regular basis. We plan to host regular 'conversations with the author' sessions, writings, and market research results about healthcare and life science industries that will not be published elsewhere. Use the QR code or link below to join the community of life science sales and marketing insiders.

thelinusgroup.com/insiders

We have all been customers. But once we're on the other side as salespeople and marketers, we immediately take on a new posture and forget all the principles of communication we use in other aspects of our lives.

So, whether you've spent your career in sales or marketing in life science or healthcare or you're just starting your career in such technical fields, this book is for you to stack the odds of the business bets you'll make in your favor.

And if you'd like to incorporate these principles into your team's marketing and sales approach, I regularly share new examples, applications, and insights through keynote presentations, workshops, and conferences. This is actually how Charles River Laboratories—the story you'll read about in Chapter 1—began working with my company, LINUS.

Finally, I'm always happy to hear from you. If you take the time to reach out, I promise I'll always personally reply.

Everything in Commercial Strategy is a Game of Psychology

What Every Single Corporate Objective Has in Common

An executive boardroom in the Back Bay, Boston

"No way."

Gina's voice tore through my nervousness as silence clung to the air. She wasn't upset or aggressive. But she was clearly not happy.

We were inside the executive offices of Charles River Laboratories, where the bustle of staccato steps outside the window on Newbury Street was the only sound reverberating inside the conference room.

Gina remained firm. "It won't work."

I inhaled a breath and pinched my eyebrows together. My company, LINUS, had spent months deep in research, synthesis, and creative exploration. The purpose of the meeting was to present our strategy for overcoming the challenges our client, Charles River Laboratories, had asked us to solve.

Gina sensed my unease. "Let me clarify. I believe both the strategy and the execution hypothesis are on target. But what you are proposing has never been done before for a reason. Our clients are biopharmaceutical companies. As much as I would love to approach them to see if they'll want to be part of our marketing campaign, I just don't believe that they will agree. And we can't risk the success of our campaign on whether we can find a client who's willing. We don't have enough time."

Hums of agreement from the executive team began to circulate. Then, my teammate spoke.

"You're right," she said. "During the development of our recommendations, we spoke extensively about these risks and dependencies. We also tested a hypothesis regarding how pharma and biotech executives are likely to act in certain situations, and that gave us the confidence to propose this unique approach."

We had their attention. My teammate smiled, continuing her explanation. "Your clients won't want to endorse one of their service providers for a variety of reasons. But what if we flip the script? What if we weren't touting Charles River in the campaign, but instead highlighting your clients' impact and the care they're providing to patients?"

The CEO's posture changed, then he said, "Caring is part of our company's culture."

As the CEO and a longtime employee, he took great pride in the role Charles River Laboratories. played in creating life-saving treatments, protecting the environment, and operating with integrity. Recently, Charles River had committed itself to global citizenship by supporting charitable causes.

"Still," he continued. "I'm not sure our clients will want to participate. But it's an intriguing idea. What do you think, Gina?"

Gina said, "Let's give it a try."

I exhaled for the first time in what felt like 15 minutes. "Great," I said, barely containing my excitement. "We will get started by recruiting some of your clients, but we will also develop a robust strategy in case we're not gaining traction."

We shook hands, concluded the meeting, and began working on this once-in-a-lifetime opportunity, one that had never been solved in life science: how to convince customers in the pharmaceutical industry to participate in marketing for one of their service providers and do it in a way that met Charles River Laboratories' marketing objective.

The Charles River Story

Charles River Laboratories is a global, full-service research organization that serves biopharmaceutical, biotech, and academic institutions. Founded as a one-person lab in 1947, the company was preparing to celebrate its 70th anniversary when we began to work together.

Charles River Laboratories' history has taken several interesting turns. After solidifying their reputation as a leading research facility, the company was sold to Bausch & Lomb in 1984. It was bought back by the founder's son, Jim Foster, thirteen years after being acquired. As the new CEO, Jim immediately began implementing a growth strategy by developing new capabilities to serve the evolving needs of the industry.

The result? Charles River Laboratories is now one of the world's most sophisticated, full-service preclinical research organizations, earning over $4.1 billion in annual revenue with more than 130 facilities globally in 2024. Additionally, they have worked on over 80% of the FDA-approved drugs over the last several years.

But a side effect of Charles River Laboratories own success was that rapid growth, market expansion, and rapid addition of services left audiences puzzled about who the company was, what it stood for, and the full suite of services it provided.

The company's leaders felt that the upcoming 70th anniversary was the perfect platform to reorient the market's perception and show their customers the entire portfolio of services that they provided.

When Perception Limits Potential

A common misconception with branding is that the company who owns the brand decides the brand's perception. In reality, the opposite is true. While businesses construct stories, it's the company's public (customers, investors, employees, and the broader industry or community in which the company operates) that ultimately determines a brand's perception.

A customer's first touchpoint with a brand often becomes the entire brand in their eyes, making it far more challenging to break this narrow impression as the company offers additional new offerings.

The general market overwhelmingly associated the Charles River Laboratories brand with its original offerings. This had obvious business implications, since current and potential customers weren't considering Charles River Laboratories for the vast suite of offerings and services they now provided.

I had been invited to give a talk for Charles River's marketing department, where I had met Gina, their chief marketing officer. After my presentation, she graciously invited me to have coffee with her. It was during this meeting that she explained their marketing challenges.

"The most common phrase we hear from customers is, 'I didn't know you offered that,'" she said, sipping her Americano. "We want to change this dynamic so the market knows the full breadth of what we offer."

She brightened. "Actually, our 70th anniversary is coming up. I think that's the perfect time to change the narrative."

I nodded. "That's a great idea. Let's schedule a time to talk about this further."

We coordinated dates, and I began putting together a series of probing questions. While I did agree with the timing, Gina and I discussed how to avoid the sophomoric "one-stop shop" message that too many healthcare and life science organizations adopt as they grow.

"In my experience, it doesn't work because it's been used too many times in our industry and doesn't convey why audiences should care. We need to give them a reason to care," I explained.

Gina nodded. Our objective was set, and we began our research.

Digging for the Truth

Charles River Laboratories is a Contract Research Organization, or CRO—a class of specialized service providers that biopharma and biotech companies hire to handle a portion of their research toward new therapies. Once seen as just a small part of the drug discovery and development process, many CROs have evolved into advanced partners that offer a wide and sophisticated range of technologies and services.

Today, Charles River Laboratories offers strategic offerings with significant technology advances and revolutionary intellectual property to deliver unique value to their clientele. They have amassed an extensive portfolio of distinctive testing, analysis, and research capabilities, which have helped them become a leader in pharmaceutical development.

When my team and I spoke to the Charles River team about their work, I was impressed by their passion. They took immense pride in the innovation that they had developed, which offered a superior level of client service.

We got to work, beginning our investigation with qualitative research by conducting in-depth interviews with target audiences. This type of research is critical; it's how we remain empathetic to scientific and healthcare audiences: **by truly understanding them and remembering what it's like to be on the other side of a sales pitch.**

In our research processes, we dig past surface-level observations and formulate, or "achieve," an insight. For Charles River Laboratories, the insight we achieved was truly powerful: pharma executives didn't fully trust their service providers.

Of course, they never directly said this.

But we would have never known this if we didn't go beyond the conversations about capabilities, evaluations, turnaround times, costs, and all the other surface-level observations.

An actionable insight is as potent as having a powerful secret about your market. Having unveiled the emotional landscape of their relationship with service providers, we knew we held the secret to developing an effective story and the potential to create a whole new conversation in the industry. It was time to craft a persuasive story for Charles River.

It was not a lack of audience awareness or interest in Charles River Laboratories or its services that needed to be fixed. It was a misperception about the company's services. We needed to create an experience to generate an urgent reason for audiences to care enough to rediscover Charles River's full value on their own.

Now that we had a secret insight about how target audiences felt about their CRO provider, we used it to guide our strategy and build our story.

Based on our research, we claimed that the traditional outsourcing dynamic was undermining the success of drug discovery and development. Even better, we had plenty of evidence to support our claim:

1. Dynamics such as study-centrism, or an overfocus on individual tasks, ignored the bigger picture items that centered the customer.
2. Prolific outsourcing had created an oversaturation of CROs, who were forced to lower their prices to compete with the demand.
3. The rise of venture-backed biopharmas (startups funded by investors) and biotech companies was creating significant bandwidth pressures on CROs, resulting in rushed, lower-quality work from some providers.

Finally, our strategy was to demonstrate that Charles River Laboratories is redefining the pharma/CRO relationship by putting their clients—and their clients' mission—at the center of everything that they do.

Bringing the Hypothesis to Life

It's virtually impossible to get someone to change their mind about something by providing facts and figures. The prefrontal cortex, the part of the brain responsible for reasoning and speech, is the path of highest resistance if you're trying to drive behavior change. That is why in life science and healthcare, sloganeering often fails.

We understood this prior to partnering with Charles River Laboratories and knew that clever art and copy were not going to articulate their value proposition thoroughly. So, instead, we chose to *demonstrate* their value proposition by letting audiences *experience it firsthand*, rather than being told.

Every company in every service-related industry claims to be a partner to their customers and clients. Our foundation for execution was to demonstrate partnership by placing Charles River Laboratories and their clients side-by-side in a joint quest to save patients' lives.

Figure 1-1: The concept board to illustrate our strategy for Charles River Laboratories' sharing the same commitment to the patient as their clients. Reproduced with permission.

Just as the Charles River Laboratories team had wisely predicted, their biopharma clients and customers were reluctant to participate in a marketing campaign that signaled an overt endorsement of their service provider. So, instead of starting with the biopharma clients, we first focused on finding amazing stories about patients whose lives had been altered because of the work that biopharma companies and Charles River had done together.

That's how we met Ginger.

Ginger, a single mom and professional jazz singer, had been diagnosed with non-small cell lung cancer, which had stolen her beautiful singing voice and threatened to shorten her life.

The biopharma company, AstraZeneca, makers of the biologic Tagrisso˚, had worked with Charles River Laboratories to fast-track the drug's FDA approval process in time to administer the therapeutic to Ginger.

The results were even better than expected. Not only had Ginger's health improved, but she had her life and voice back.

Having received permission from all parties involved, we set out to tell the world Ginger's story at that year's Lung Cancer Congress in Vienna, Austria. We invited Ginger, her oncologist, her care providers, and scientists from AstraZeneca and Charles River Laboratories to a private event, where Ginger performed a concert for the team that fought to get her voice back.

We selected a gorgeous venue: an old factory with floor-to-ceiling glass windows that amplified Ginger's voice as it enveloped us all in gratitude.

Because everyone there helped her reclaim her voice. They were present for her battle.

Every voice.

Every fight.

Every step of the way.

And the entire experience was captured on film.

Figure 1-2: Outdoor advertising at the New York Stock Exchange to promote the first short film about Charles River Laboratories' role in how Ginger got her voice back.

This intimate moment genuinely demonstrated the positive impact that Charles River Laboratories had played a part with its client, AstraZeneca, in the lives of its patients. Ginger's powerful story illustrated the company's promise, values, offerings, and most importantly, alignment with the ultimate goal of their clientele.

With Charles Rivers' marketing and communications team, we developed a multi-channel campaign.

In the first six weeks of launching Ginger's story, our campaign garnered 12 million impressions, with direct connection to an interactive description of all the services that Charles River's team had provided to their pharma client to move the therapeutic through the FDA process.

Having performed a baseline brand study just prior to the launch of this initiative, we benchmarked the brand a year later to see significant changes in the target audience's understanding and perception of Charles River Laboratories in the market, which found a large increase in the number of respondents who claimed to be working with the company for the first time. Additionally, Charles River Laboratories' internal morale had continued to improve, with employees reporting pride in their company.

Situating the Story

I love my team. Although the Charles River Laboratories' story does showcase how incredibly talented they are, the purpose of this book isn't to show off our work or accomplishments.

Instead, it's meant to describe the simple yet powerful frameworks and techniques you can use to reach your own goals by identifying and minimizing barriers, whether your goals are related to fundraising, hiring, marketing, or sales. Why? Because reaching these goals all have one thing in common.

Virtually every corporate objective in every company depends on people to take action:

- Want to increase revenue? Customers need to take a series of actions that lead to purchasing and adoption.

- Need to raise capital? Investors need to take action to meet with you, evaluate your company, and then provide you with funding.
- Want to grow? Current employees need to take action to execute their jobs efficiently, while prospective employees must first quit their current roles and then accept your offer.

All of these dependencies rely on orchestrating others to take action.

Though intellectually simple to understand, it should be immediately apparent why corporate objectives are so difficult to achieve: people don't take actions based on logic alone, and only a small portion of people take action because they are told or forced to. People's actions are governed by their psychology, and they follow specific patterns in how they respond to stimuli.

In the coming chapters, I will present concepts and frameworks for sales and marketing in life science and healthcare to develop highly effective commercial strategies that transcend the mediocrity of traditional efforts. I will do this by deconstructing the Charles River Laboratories case study further and providing additional examples that illustrate the power of this framework for persuading scientists, doctors, and other technical professionals.

Let's get started.

CHAPTER 2

How Technical Professionals Make Decisions

Synopsis

As consumers, technical professionals—scientists, doctors, engineers, and other professionals who make decisions in a technical environment or hold degrees in math, science, or medicine—all have two things in common:

1. They are more skeptical than average decision-makers.
2. They follow a very specific and predictable pattern in making decisions.

Technical professionals are trained to make decisions based on facts, data, and evidence. But while they pride themselves on rationality, their decision-making is still subject to the same psychological biases, social influences, and emotional undercurrents that shape all human behavior. The difference lies in how these forces are expressed.

This chapter explores the psychology behind how technical professionals think, process information, and make commercial decisions. Throughout this book, the term *technical professionals* will refer to this audience while *commercial teams* refers to the sales and marketing executives, directors, managers, and individual contributors who work to reach them.

In this chapter, we will discuss:

- Why the assumption of purely rational decision-making is flawed
- The three types of benefits that people seek to actually drive their decision
- The two dimensions of decision-making and how technical professionals are unique
- Why traditional commercial strategies often fail to connect
- How understanding cognitive processes leads to more effective communication and influence

My goal is not to critique the analytical mindset, but to understand it and to put you in a better position for persuading your target customers. We will explore the specific model for persuasion in the next chapter.

Rational Myth

For decades, commercial teams have assumed that technical professionals make purely rational, data-driven decisions. After all, survey after survey of scientists and doctors reinforced this, as they constantly ask for more data, more evidence, and more proof. "Just show me the data," they often say. This belief shapes everything from marketing materials to sales presentations, which are often loaded with data, specifications, and dense technical claims. Yet, despite these efforts, influencing them with data often stalls.

The truth is that technical professionals are rational, but they are also human. Their training teaches them to evaluate data objectively, but their interpretations are influenced by personal experience, professional identity, and social proof within their community.

Consider a scientist choosing between two different brands of an analytical instrument. Functionally, both brands perform the same and both instruments tout the same number of academic citations. But one seems to be used by more prominent scientists. As a buyer, the scientist will likely perceive that brand as the safer or more credible option, even if its performance metrics are identical. The decision feels rational, but it is informed by an ultimate desire for this scientist to be seen as one of the great scientists in their peer community.

This distinction matters because commercial teams often mistake information for influence. Providing more data does not necessarily lead to better persuasion, and sometimes even backfires, as technical professionals get caught in analyzing the information for academic sport, rather than motivating them to move forward. True influence requires understanding what motivates belief and how the mind processes risk, reward, and uncertainty.

Technical professionals make decisions at the intersection of their objective thinking and subjective point of view, where they evaluate the three types of benefits they seek.

Three Types of Benefits

In his book, *Building Strong Brands,* strategist David A. Aaker explained three types of benefits that people seek when making a decision, Functional, Emotional, and Self-expressive. Each of these benefits map directly to one of the three decision-making drivers. Figure 2-1 presents details of each.

Decision-Making Driver	Benefit	Question it Answers
Logic	Functional	What is the truth?
Emotion	Emotional	How will I feel?
Ego	Self-expressive	How will others view me?

Figure 2-1: The entire spectrum of benefits that commercial teams can use to resonate with their audience extends far beyond the obvious, functional benefits of a product. By employing emotional and self-expressive benefits, teams can open up entire classes of benefits for their technical offerings. For more information about the three types of benefits please see David Aaker's book, Building Stong Brands.

However, most commercial teams in life science and healthcare fall into a predictable trap. Consider how many of these phrases you've encountered:

- Better quality
- Faster turnaround time

- Do more with less
- Simple workflow
- More time

Let's face it, the list above describes the vast majority of "value propositions" in healthcare and life science and probably most other products and services that your audience is exposed to today. If an average scientist or doctor is conservatively exposed to 100 of such messages every day, it's easy to see how quickly these statements lose any meaning, no matter how cute or clever their delivery.

Most commercial efforts for technical offerings tout logical feature-benefit statements. While appealing to logic is necessary in healthcare and life science, commercial teams usually don't succeed in breaking through the noise, let alone generate meaningful demand within their audience if they ignore *emotion* and *ego*.

To be clear, I am not proposing empty emotional statements about saving the world or over-romanticizing the moment of scientific discovery, as they usually solicit nothing more than eyerolls.

The key is to know *when* and *how* to engage the audience's logic, emotion, and ego during their own buying journey, which for technical professionals, has an additional dimension than for other audiences. Luckily, the patterns in their behavior give us a proverbial map we can follow.

Mapping How Technical Professionals Make Buying Decisions

Like all people, technical professionals rely on both logic and emotion or ego for their decision-making. They evaluate information through either an *objective* or *subjective* frame of reference. Although the technical nature of their work is based on objective evaluation of facts and evidence, their decision-making is never based solely on logic. Their subjective frame of reference significantly influences their decisions. So far, this interplay between logic and emotion and approaching information objectively and subjectively is all human nature.

There is a second dimension to how technical people make decisions: They have a keen sense of *curiosity* and *skepticism* as well, because the very nature of their work relies on these two senses. Curiosity drives a scientist to wonder why the world works in a certain way and to make novel observations, or a doctor to correctly diagnose a patient or solve a health-related problem. Skepticism keeps them from prematurely believing their observations. **In other words, they are trained to hold any piece of information in contempt until they have satisfied their own sense of skepticism.** Good luck selling against that kind of mindset.

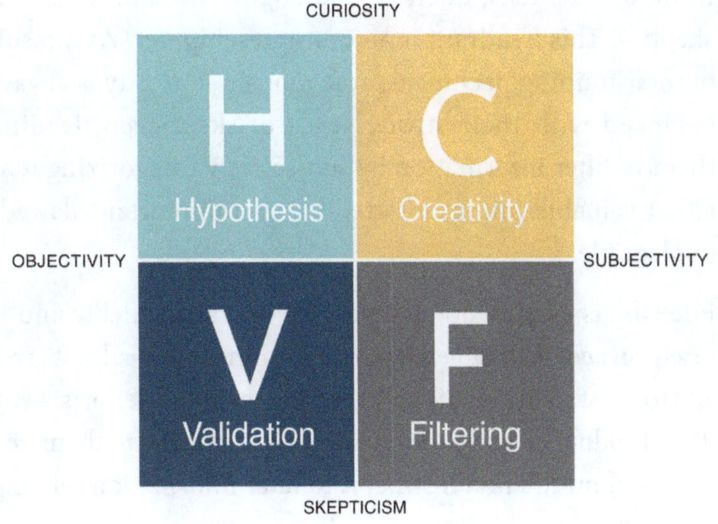

Figure 2-2: Technical professionals are constantly trading off between satisfying their curiosity and appeasing their skepticism. Also, they evaluate information using both an objective and their own subjective frames of reference. These two dynamics create a landscape of four possible modes that technical professionals navigate in real time when presented with information.

When mapped together, these two dimensions create a rich landscape to determine how technical professionals will react to information. The quadrants of the Cartesian plane above generate four narratives that describe how technical professionals consume information and the outcome for how they are likely to act.

Subjective Skepticism Leads to Filtering

This lower-right quadrant, where technical professionals' subjectivity and skepticism intersect, is the reason why we think of scientists, doctors, and engineers as professional skeptics. This quadrant is an omnipresent *filter*. As a result of their training, technical professionals' curiosity is always balanced with their strong sense of skepticism, leading them to filter information by subjectively categorizing it as either valuable/important/credible or unimportant/flawed/implausible.

Filtering is usually not objective. It operates quickly and is rarely turned off completely. And activating this quadrant gives end to most well-intentioned sales and marketing efforts. Even if the product or service is quantifiably beneficial to them, the technical mind's first instinct is to filter information relating to a pitch.

Subjective Curiosity Leads to Creativity

The upper right quadrant is activated when technical professionals react to a stimulus (i.e., a publication, a conversation, or any sort of content) that makes them curious and somehow resonates with them subjectively. In this state, their minds are most open and free and thinking associatively, considering "what if" scenarios about their work. This quadrant is very exciting; it's where a technical professional's intuition, instinct, excitement, and the beginning of a scientific journey are formed. It is also where they begin their decision journey.

With a flush of dopamine coursing through their brains, these professionals have a creative thought that is so powerful and gripping that they would be willing to dedicate their lives to prove out that thought. This is why they fail every day for years, or even decades, resulting in endless experiments, because they made science personal. And invoking this same feeling is the key to start them in their purchasing decision journey. I will show you how in the next chapter.

Objective Curiosity Leads to a Hypothesis

Technical professionals spend much of their time operating through an objective frame of reference. When they are curious and apply objectivity to their thinking, they form hypotheses that will encourage them to engage further in the information that will lead them toward validation or rejection of their hypothesis. Technical professionals rarely expend the energy to form a hypothesis if they haven't had a creative thought, and they won't act on next steps until they've formed a rigorous hypothesis.

However, the hypothesis needs to be of their own formation, not handed to them, because it will otherwise prematurely invoke their sense of skepticism and result in filtering. In this state, they look for information that will allow them to form their own hypothesis.

Objective Skepticism Leads to Validation

Once a hypothesis is established, technical professionals move to the lower-left quadrant to objectively satisfy their skepticism. This is where most technical professionals exert most of their energy, repeatedly trying to validate their hypothesis by evaluating until they feel certain that they have reached the truth. They filter out biased or unimportant information until they have proven to themselves that their observations are real.

While I have described these quadrants as discrete and in linear order, the technically trained mind can dwell anywhere in this landscape and rapidly shift from one state to another. The key for sales and marketing teams in healthcare or life science is to determine how to navigate this landscape by appropriately engaging and/or suppressing the pertinent quadrants according to where their audience or buyer is, and what they are seeking to achieve to move their own decision forward.

Now that we have a specific map for how technical professionals react to information, we can now build a specific and actionable journey for how they buy.

The Technical Buying Journey

Technical professionals generally follow a three-phase path in purchasing products or services. This is different from sales cycles, which are seller-centric. The technical buying journey is led by the customers themselves.

The three phases are *Recognition, Exploration*, and *Evaluation*. The goal of commercial teams should be to understand the phases as they relate to their audience and develop compelling content and experiences, or stimuli, that move their audience swiftly from phase to phase in their own buying journeys.

Figure 2-3: Technical professionals typically follow three phases in their buying journey, with pertinent states of thought activated as shown. This model holds true for virtually every product category in healthcare and life science.

It's simpler than it sounds but filled with opportunity. Let's break down each phase:

Recognition

Contrary to popular belief, the buying journey does not start with awareness. It starts with the technical professional's own *recognition* of a need or an opportunity.

Needs and opportunities are often latent, meaning that they already exist but are buried deep in the target audience's minds. Most of the time, needs remain latent through unconscious inertia or habits that compensate for less-than-ideal processes. Yet once technical professionals consciously recognize a need or an opportunity, their creativity is activated, and they embark on a buying journey.

Helping a target audience recognize a need represents the most powerful way to captivate a technical professional's attention. **Regardless of the product or service being offered and regardless of the company's reach or strength, the audience's need is the most powerful activator of curiosity, and the best way for commercial teams to instill intent to buy in their audience.** Articulating an unmet or unseen need can move audiences from "not looking" to becoming actively "on the market." The first job in developing any commercial strategy should therefore be to create *recognition* of a need in the minds of the audience.

At this phase of the buying journey, the audience is likely to have a creative thought, which results in a dopamine release and motivates them to the next phase of their buying journey.

Exploration

When technical professionals recognize that they have a need, they begin to explore.

Cognitively, they are looking to form a hypothesis about the best way to satisfy their need or take advantage of a newly recognized opportunity, but psychologically, they are looking for a shortcut (called a heuristic) to minimize the effort to move forward. This phase is purely explorative; it's about the potential to fulfill a need, with no restrictions or definitions as to how this might be achieved.

To form an objective hypothesis about how to solve a problem, technical professionals typically engage with content or experiences that they deem factual and credible, and filter out information that attempts to sway their hypothesis. In this phase technical professionals are looking to form a hypothesis, not make a decision or get into action yet. Only after they have explored will they confidently move toward action.

Evaluation

Only once technical professionals have completed their exploration and have formulated a hypothesis about the best way to satisfy their need they recognize, do they begin to evaluate specific products and services.

This may be the first time audiences overtly engage with companies about their products and services. And while they are looking for the best option, they are actually looking to validate their hypothesis.

As every healthcare and life science sales professional will attest, technical professionals in this phase look at much more than the full capabilities of the product or service offering, no matter how technical. They try to mentally rehearse the experience of being a company's customer before actually purchasing from the company or becoming an active prescriber. Cognitively, they do this through requests for demonstrations, site visits, experimental data on their own samples, or for evidence about efficacy.

At the same time, they subconsciously sense what it may be like to do business with the company through evaluating the sum total of all interactions. In this phase of the buying journey, technical professionals use all their senses as they gear up to finalize their purchase decision.

Descriptive, but not Prescriptive

Technical professionals are deliberate decision-makers, evaluating their options through both logic and emotion and driven by their highly refined sense of curiosity and skepticism. Their skepticism is not a barrier but an invitation to meet them where they are, with empathy for the information they crave at different stages of their buying journey.

So many traditional sales and marketing efforts fail because they treat technical professionals as subjects to be rendered into submission through the best logical arguments and treat their skepticism as resistance rather than discernment. By understanding how the technically trained mind processes information and risk, commercial teams can design strategies that feel relevant, human, and respectful.

If you find this information interesting but aren't sure what to do with it, I don't blame you. The first time I presented this model about how technical professionals make decisions to a group of sales and marketing executives, they all shared this sentiment. Like you, they wanted to know what to do.

The next chapter builds on this foundation. It explores how to move from understanding decision-making to persuade technical professionals ethically and effectively through an Insights-Led Model for Commercial Strategy.

CHAPTER 3

Persuading Technical Professionals: A Model for Commercial Strategies

Synopsis

Understanding how technical professionals make decisions is only half the challenge. The next step is learning how to influence those decisions.

This chapter introduces a practical model that connects behavioral psychology to commercial strategy. It explains how influence operates in complex technical markets and provides a framework for developing strategies and messaging that move technical audiences to act. I call this model the Insights-Led Model for Commercial Strategy.

In this chapter, you will learn:

- Why traditional persuasion usually fails in technical markets
- The buying journey that technical professionals take

- The three pillars of persuasive commercial strategy
- What encompasses an Insights-Led Model for Commercial Strategy

Why Your Audience is Not Buying It

Now that you've seen how the mind of a technical professional really works and what they're truly after in each stage of their decision-making, I'm sure it is apparent why today's traditional commercial strategies are ineffective. Well-intentioned messages that tout the benefits of an offering prematurely push this audience into a validation mindset, or worse, activate their filters outright.

Consumer marketing and B2B strategies claim that audiences need to become aware of a product and what it can do for them, and then they will desire it. This may work in non-technical B2B markets, but for a technical audience, the barrier is not that they do not know about an offering, it is that they do not care. So even when launching a new scientific or medical product or service, the role of the commercial team is to first make the audience care and then to persuade them.

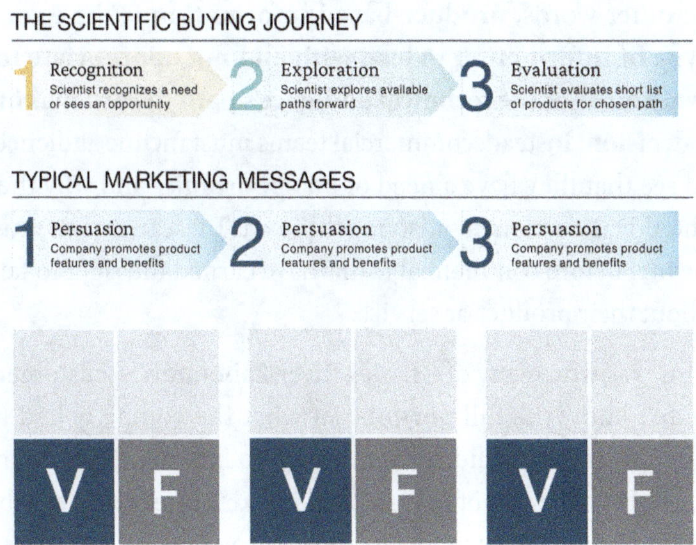

Figure 3-1: Typical messaging strategies ubiquitously promote product features and benefits and fail to adapt content to the technical buying journey. This has a counterproductive effect and heightens the audience's skepticism.

If technical professionals do not want a product, it means they have not yet recognized their need for it and thus filter any information presented about any product, effectively rendering any offers or promotions useless at this stage.

Even if they have recognized a need or an opportunity and are in the Exploration phase, technically trained minds are in the process of forming a hypothesis. They are more likely to be attracted to information they have identified as credible and want to make their own hypothesis rather than being told the answer or told what to do.

In other words, **product-based information is the wrong type of information to lead with and not appropriate for two-thirds of the technical audience's path toward making a decision.** Instead, commercial teams must incline audiences to see that they have a need or an opportunity and why they should take action in satisfying the need. These two goals must be met before commercial teams have earned the right to talk about their product or service.

This was why many of Charles River Laboratories' customers didn't know the full portfolio of what the company had to offer: they simply didn't care enough to find out. No amount of effort on the part of the sales and marketing team to describe all the company's wonderful services would have inspired their audience to care enough to engage with Charles River Laboratories differently.

Persuading Technical Professionals: A Model Buying Journey

Now that we have established a predictable pattern for how technical professionals make decisions and why traditional commercial efforts are often misaligned with this pattern, let us explore a buying journey that will serve as the foundation of commercial strategies for technical B2B offerings such as scientific, medical and healthcare products and services.

As we established in Chapter 2 technical professionals go through three phases in making a decision: Recognition, Exploration, and Evaluation.

In the Recognition phase, commercial teams must spark creativity in their audience by giving them the ingredients to have a "what if" moment. In the Exploration phase, teams must inspire technical professionals to formulate a hypothesis about that "what if" thought. And in the Evaluation phase, commercial teams must enable them to validate their own hypothesis, to see that with the right offering their "what if" idea can become reality.

At each phase of the buying journey, companies must design and develop discrete types of stimuli, ones intended to spark creativity, others to help audiences formulate hypotheses, and finally ones to enable validation. In commercial terms, stimuli can be anything that is experienced by the audience, ranging from things they read to an experience they have, online or offline. All marketing and sales content are stimuli for audiences.

We call this the Insights-Led Model for Commercial Strategy and outline three types of stimuli: Leadership, Education, and Persuasion. Each facet of the model will be capitalized throughout this book for ease of reference.

This model provides a universal template for commercial teams to send the right message through each type of stimuli at the right time in the buying journey through their sales and marketing channels.

THE SCIENTIFIC BUYING JOURNEY

1 Recognition
Scientist recognizes a need
or sees an opportunity

2 Exploration
Scientist explores available
paths forward

3 Evaluation
Scientist evaluates short list
of products for chosen path

OPTIMUM MARKETING MESSAGES

1 Leadership
Have a compelling point
of view about an issue

2 Education
Provide background
information about the issue

3 Persuasion
Simulate the customer
experience

Figure 3-2: There are three critical classes of stimuli needed to effectively engage technical professionals. The goal of marketing campaigns should be to eliminate barriers for scientists as they move from one phase of their buying journey to the next by providing them the type of information they are open to at each phase.

Let's take a deeper dive into each type of stimuli, to see how these will serve as the foundation of your commercial strategy.

Leadership Stimuli: Driving Recognition of a Need

As of this writing, the main conversation that dominates the market for DNA sequencers revolves around three factors: the cost of sequencing a genome, the accuracy of different sequencing technologies, and novel capabilities to open up sample input or the ability to see the difference in the sequence of single cells within a sample.

As you can surmise, these factors are sometimes in tension with each other. Now imagine two advertisements for the same DNA sequencing system. One headline reads: *Achieve the Highest Accuracy with Long-Read Sequencing,* paired with imagery, copy, sample data, a call to action, and corporate branding. The second advertisement is nothing more than a provocative statement: *Your Current Sequencer is Looking for a Needle in a Stack of Needles*, then goes on to talk about wasting resources associated with a less accurate sequencing system. Both ads provide a URL. Which ad do you think is more effective at generating action? Which will pique the curiosity of the genomics community to explore the story behind the ad? If you guessed the second ad, then you're correct.

During the Recognition phase of the technical buying journey, commercial teams need to gain the attention of their audience and spark creativity. Instead of providing visual impact or aiming to inform the audience, **marketers and salespeople need to display an act of leadership by staking a claim on the audience's needs.** A thought-provoking statement or question that takes a stance about an issue the audience is facing effectively sparks their curiosity, helping them recognize that they have a need or may be missing an opportunity. Awareness is created as a result, but this awareness is the recognition of a need or an opportunity, not about a product or a service.

Even audiences who disagree with the claim would likely be curious enough to learn more. This presents an opportunity to segment the market as those who agree with the company, and hence would be the easiest prospects to convert into customers, and those who need significant nurturing to become customers.

As illustrated by Charles River's campaign, Leadership content commands attention. In this example, we set out to claim that pharma companies and CROs deserved better relationships, and we did this by reminding the world that Charles River Laboratories shared a common goal with its audience. This effort was successful in driving recognition of a need: redefining the Pharma-CRO relationship.

But without proper justification, Leadership stimuli can be interpreted as click-bait or bravado. A true Leadership strategy needs ample evidence as to why it is relevant. This is where *Education stimuli* becomes vital.

Education Stimuli: Empowering Customers to Decide for Themselves

If a well-crafted Leadership message is successful in piquing the audience's curiosity and aiding them in recognizing that they have a need, they will instinctively take action to form their own hypothesis about whether this need is relevant to them. The next class of stimuli offered should be educational in nature, aiding the audience to explore the topic further without being sold to. Done well, Educational stimuli preconditions the audience to adopt the company's thinking.

Recalling that technical professionals keep their curiosity in check with a highly refined sense of skepticism, the job of marketers and salespeople at this phase will be to keep their audience in a state of curiosity for as long as possible. The way to accomplish this is to **encourage scientists to shift from a**

subjective to an objective frame of reference by providing evidence about why the stated need is relevant and to avoid getting into solution mode.

To infuse enough credibility into a company's Educational stimuli, commercial teams need to find reliable proxies. Since content is a main currency in professional fields, commercial teams can leverage lots of public information to reference, repackage, digest, review, analyze, synthesize, and earn attention on media channels through public relations.

Continuing with the above example of the DNA sequencer, the URL in the first ad would inevitably take audiences to a product page that gushes about the offering's features and benefits. The URL on the provocative ad, however, would direct scientists to content that illustrates the average amount of waste generated due to the gap in accuracy from conventional sequencers and compares to the true cost-per-genome. This information would then be used to generate editorial articles that clearly show the comparison and the pros and cons of each approach in different settings, along with a calculator for scientists to determine how much resource is being wasted with their own current methodologies.

Educational stimuli are the invaluable fuel that enable commercial teams to shape the way their market thinks.

In many technical fields, commercial teams produce an impressive volume of scientific or medical content, often labeled as "educational." I encounter two common misperceptions about what truly qualifies as educational content when viewed through the lens of the audience's buying journey.

The first misperception is educational content that may be of general or idle interest to the audience but does not generate intent because it does not directly situate or personalize the Leadership message. **Educational stimuli should always be in direct support of the provocation laid out by the Leadership message.** Otherwise, such stimuli may generate leads, but will never generate intent or drive action.

The second misperception concerns content like webinars that demonstrate an offering's capabilities either by featuring a third party endorsement or new application. These are often seen as thinly veiled product demonstrations, not as educational content that helps technical professionals form a hypothesis. When it comes to the buying journey of technical audiences, Educational stimuli should serve to substantiate and personalize the need articulated by the Leadership message. In an initial audit of a commercial team's content efforts, we usually find too much effort being put toward these Educational stimuli that may generate metrics, but don't move prospects forward in their buying journey.

Persuasion: Simulating the Experience of Doing Business with You

Technical professionals enter the Evaluation phase of their decision journey only after they have formed a hypothesis about the optimal path for meeting their need and the option that may win their business is the one that most closely validates their own hypothesis. This is the first time in their buying journey that technical professionals truly engage with a company's offerings with any serious attention. In this phase, information needs to be persuasive and simulate the positive experience of becoming a company's customer. Referring again to our DNA sequencer example from above, this is the phase in which scientists would be open to hearing about the possibilities and benefits of the product and learning more about how the new technology would resolve the tension between sequencing costs and the improved accuracy of their data.

The most persuasive messaging is developed from the audience's perspective, clearly demonstrating intimate knowledge of their need and avoiding hyperbole. If commercial leaders have followed their audience's own buying journey, then they have successfully predisposed their audience to make the hypothesis the company wanted them to make and now merely need to provide the necessary validation to that hypothesis. There are a few ways to optimize Persuasion stimuli.

First, it's important to remember that messages can be transmitted through multiple senses. Relying only on the logical center of the audience's brain usually represents the path of highest resistance. This means that slogans, messages, presentations, and all forms of telling technical audiences about a product's value proposition are less likely to actually persuade them. Commercial professionals would be far more effective by translating the intended Persuasion message to stimuli that demonstrate the value proposition, rather than saying it. I will cover how to do this more effectively in Chapter 7.

Second, it is not practical to develop commercial efforts without saying anything. In developing Persuasion stimuli that use statements, I advise commercial teams to minimize the rampant use of hyperbolic claims such as "innovative," "easy-to-use," or "high-quality," as they just reactivate skepticism that results in filtering. These claims don't feel credible, and they undermine the audience's trust.

Leveraging the Insights-Led Model for Commercial Strategy

The three pillars of Leadership, Education, and Persuasion messaging do not operate in sequence; they form a continuous loop of influence. Each reinforces the others, creating a complete commercial experience.

In practice, this means every commercial initiative, whether it is a product or brand launch, a growth campaign, or a market development initiative, should include elements of all three stimuli. A campaign might begin with a thought-provoking insight (Leadership), provide clear evidence and application (Education), and culminate in an interactive validation experience (Persuasion). Commercial teams need to be ready to engage with audiences wherever they are in the buying journey, rather than beginning every interaction with a product pitch.

When these elements are unified, the audience perceives the overall value proposition. They see a company that not only understands their world but moves seamlessly between intellect, evidence, and experience. That coherence builds trust, and trust drives adoption.

A life science company once faced a familiar problem: despite strong technology and a solid flow of leads in a market development initiative, they suffered a massive drop-off of activity in the mid-funnel. Through a sales empowerment initiative, we discovered that their audience were facing two internal struggles in their own decision journey:

1. They found it difficult to gain internal championship and alignment for the purchase.
2. They were overwhelmed by the effort to make a switch from one vendor to another, because each vendor required different site prep and data regimes.

When we looked at the company's Education content, we found an overabundance of scientific demonstrations about the product's quality and zero content addressing the actual issues that were holding their interested prospects from making a purchase. We redesigned their campaign to articulate a strong Leadership message and focused on a step-by-step guide for gaining internal consensus and site prep. From a pure numbers perspective, engagement declined slightly, but mid-funnel throughput rose 20x, leading to much better commercial outcomes.

The power of the Insights-Led Model for Commercial Strategy lies in its discipline. It does not chase trends or tools. It aligns psychology with practice, evidence with empathy, and messaging with meaning.

Commercial executives and teams sometimes ask if the Insights-Led Model for Commercial Strategy is applicable for all technical products. More specifically, many commercial teams wonder if such a model will be effective for products with little to no technical differentiation (I don't believe in such a thing as a commodity in our market, only products that have not been differentiated yet). In these situations, it might be tempting to rely on hype or media weight to drill a boastful message into the market. But experienced commercial teams know empty tactics serve only to increase noise and seldom make substantive difference in the market's acceptance of a product.

While at first glance it may seem difficult to market an offering that lacks a lockout or differentiating feature, consumer industries have demonstrated the power of clever positioning, even with no functional differentiator. I have successfully used insights-led commercial strategies for the entire spectrum of situations, ranging from highly technical instruments or services to small plasticware to successful investor pitches and even employer brands. **The key is to escape the boundaries of functional benefits and leverage the complete spectrum of the decision drivers of technical professionals.**

Practically every product is marketable. The key to a successful insights-led strategy will be to find a latent need that, once recognized, will lead the audience to the product's doorstep. By keeping the customer at the center of this process, commercial teams need to achieve actionable insights about their audiences, paint a truthful picture of a positive experience, and ultimately shape the market by dominating the conversation.

The Most Critical Ingredient to Succeed in Insights-Led Model for Commercial Strategy: The Secret

It's one thing to observe that scientists favor one particular brand of DNA sequencers over another. It's another thing to achieve the insight that these scientists fear being seen as second-class and that owning the brand of sequencer favored by their peers delivers a self-expressive benefit to them. Not one scientist we interviewed for a client said this to us. Instead, they all displayed it in the way they rationalized the tensions we presented to them. Watching them perform rationalization gymnastics and even go as far as apologizing for a brand that they had just told us they despised was the door that let us peer into their deepest secret: that they feared not being seen as good enough within their professional community of peers. Every commercial strategy needs this kind of a secret to be powerful. This type of secret is a true insight.

In the context of commercial strategy, an insight is a deep, non-obvious understanding of customer behavior, motivation, or dynamic that can shape how a business communicates, sells, competes, and delivers value. It is not just a statement of fact or a reflection of what customers are doing; it is a reframing of what drives those actions, often revealing an emotional or psychological truth that isn't immediately visible. A strong insight has the potential to fundamentally change the effectiveness of all strategic or tactical decisions that can shift both marketing and sales approaches in more effective and resonant ways. It's the secret to unlocking and shaping the market.

Most commercial strategies in healthcare and life science don't achieve deep insights about the audience they are selling to, and as a result, they are subject to the natural market forces. Instead, they rely on internal team experience, market trends, or market research reports.

Insights are different from market trends, which are broad patterns that predict the growth of a market in the next few years or general rise in demands for needs such as sustainable packaging. Insights also differ from classic market research, such as survey data focus group responses or usage statistics. Such observations might tell you that "65% of scientists make decisions on which sequencer to purchase because of the cost-per-genome price" but they don't explain what buyers are really seeking in that experience.

These trends or patterns observations are all important for understanding the larger direction of the market, but they rarely get to the emotional or situational drivers that influence an individual customer's decision-making or pave the way on how to generate high-intent prospects. Insights are narrower in focus but deeper in meaning. They don't just tell you what's happening: **they reveal why it matters and how your customer will act when presented with a particular situation.**

Now that the conceptual framework has been introduced, we need to examine how your insights fit within the broader competitive landscape. In the next section we systematically examine how to develop a winning commercial strategy by performing four analyses: situation analysis, achieving insight, and the two sides of the product-market fit (the product side and the market side). These analyses will provide the foundational information that commercial teams need to develop a strong insights-led commercial strategy. In the last section of this book, I will provide specifics on how to execute such strategies and significantly increase your commercial outcomes.

The Secrets You Need to Master the Game of Psychology

CHAPTER 4

Situation Analysis: Landscaping the Competitive Market

Synopsis

In any campaign guided by the Insights-Led Model for Commercial Strategy, effective decision-making begins with a clear, structured understanding of the market's dynamics. But in complex, technical fields, many commercial teams operate on assumptions, surface-level data, or an overfocusing on competitors. This chapter outlines how to conduct a rigorous and nuanced situation analysis, which is a foundational step that informs the development of strategies rooted in true customer insight.

In this chapter, you will learn how to:

- Map the marketplace using three critical vantage points
- Conduct internal stakeholder interviews and perform honest SWOT (Strengths, Weaknesses, Opportunities, and Threats) analyses

- Analyze competitive positioning through attribute mapping
- Apply the technology adoption lifecycle to understand market readiness
- Use qualitative research techniques to uncover latent customer needs that are not captured in traditional data

By the end of this chapter, you will have a clear process for turning raw information into actionable insight and a practical framework for making your commercial strategy more aligned, competitive, and effective.

Three Vantage Points of the Landscape

To achieve meaningful insights for commercial strategy, we must first perform situation analysis, which entails developing a structured map of the marketplace.

Situation analysis is approached a little differently across healthcare and life science sectors. While both sectors often start with market size and growth data, healthcare companies are more likely to dig into their audiences' attitudes, perceptions, behaviors, and needs. In contrast, life science and diagnostics offerings are sometimes so scientific that they require technically trained teams who often rely on their own experiences to understand their target customers. Frequently this is at the expense of formal audience analysis.

Skipping structured investigation of the audience's reality often limits strategic depth. The most effective commercial strategies begin by answering one question: **Why should a specific audience care?** The answer lies at the intersection of three vantage points: *dynamics within the company, the competition, and the customer.* Situation analysis is the map that helps you find it.

Only by objectively viewing the situation through all three of these lenses can you uncover insights that lead to strategy. When viewed independently, each lens offers partial clarity; when combined, they form the foundation of an Insights-Led Model for Commercial Strategy.

Company Dynamics

This perspective focuses on how the organization perceives itself: its capabilities, constraints, beliefs, and aspirations. It includes a realistic evaluation of what the company can credibly offer and the barriers it needs to overcome. A key tool here is the **SWOT analysis**. Although at first blush this tool seems outdated or basic, it is a worthwhile tool for commercial teams. However, for its value to be realized, commercial teams must be committed to using it with rigorous honesty. Many companies fall into the trap of treating it as a performative exercise, by bashing the competition or by minimizing their weaknesses. Instead, a powerful SWOT analysis should serve as a mirror that reflects intrinsic competencies and the headwinds or tailwinds shaping the business.

As Figure 4-1 illustrates, the top two quadrants in a typical SWOT assessment—strengths and weaknesses—are *intrinsic positives and negatives,* meaning that they are ultimately within the control of the company itself. Conversely, the lower quadrants—opportunities and threats—are *extrinsic positives and negatives* and are outside of the company's control.

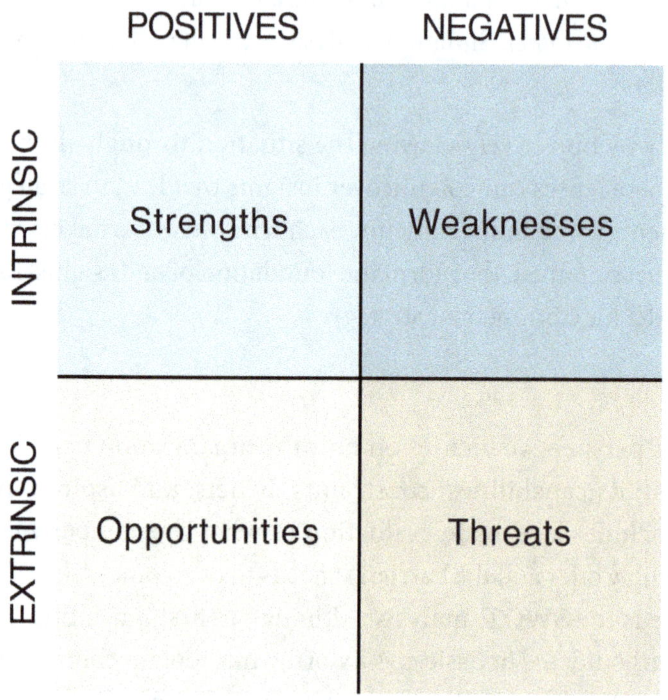

Figure 4-1: SWOT analysis requires careful delineation between factors that are within or outside of the company's control.

Many times, commercial teams confuse strengths with opportunities and weaknesses with threats. The key is to investigate whether a particular dynamic is truly within or outside of the company's control. This confusion is no one's fault. Differentiating between an opportunity and a strength or a threat and a weakness can vary by perspective and is confusing by default. If a competitor has a bigger brand and a similar product, is that a weakness or a threat?

Consider the below example where you are performing SWOT analysis for a pipette manufacturer with two competitors:

- Competitor A is a life science company developing pipettes. They are a small, family-owned company.
- Competitor B is a life science company that also develops pipettes, along with various lab equipment. They are a large, well-known company.

The products are identical in use and appearance. Is it an opportunity for you that Competitor A is smaller, or is it a threat because they may be able to serve their customers more intimately? Similarly, is it a threat to you that Competitor B has the same product, along with others, and a bigger audience, or is that an opportunity for you to demonstrate your focus?

Companies can't control the competition. But companies can control their own products and how they respond to the competition.

Additionally, a bigger brand does not necessarily mean a better brand. Companies are frequently acquired by bigger companies in the life science industry, which can muddle their audience's perceptions. Smaller companies can absolutely develop magnificent brands as well.

A SWOT exercise, guided by data, becomes a bridge between perception and reality. It can highlight tensions within the organization itself—for instance, a brand that sees itself as innovative but is actually risk-averse in practice or a team that aspires to launch breakthrough solutions but is measured on incremental Key Performance Indicators (KPIs). The point is not to surface every possible factor but to isolate the ones most meaningful to strategic differentiation.

Competitive Dynamics

Once commercial teams have internal clarity, the next step is to understand the competitive terrain. Every commercial team must thoroughly analyze the external forces in play. Mapping how competitors position themselves in the market allows us to identify not just who we're up against, but how they're communicating value. A useful method for this is **attribute analysis**: categorizing and quantifying the features and messages used by each competitor. These can be visualized using tools like spider graphs or heat maps to highlight areas of overlap and differentiation.

For example, therapeutics may position themselves primarily on efficacy, diagnostics on accuracy and turnaround time, and scientific tools on workflow integration. While many companies enumerate all possible attributes in their messaging, it is the selective emphasis that reveals strategic intent. Observing not just what competitors say, but what they omit, can uncover underutilized angles.

For example, in the market for laboratory centrifuges, if Company A emphasizes maximum speed, Company B highlights temperature range, and Company C focuses on noise level, Company D that can credibly own a workflow-simplification narrative may find itself alone in a high-value space.

Understanding the complete competitive landscape requires expansion beyond direct competitors and inclusion of other product categories, services, or processes that may satisfy a particular need for audiences. The first key question to be answered is thus: *Against whom and with what does the offering compete?*

It is important to identify **non-obvious competition**. One startup offering cloud-based lab notebooks assumed their competitors were other digital platforms. However, through market analysis and field interviews, we discovered that the primary competitor was still paper notebooks. While all of the other competitors were positioning themselves against each other, the startup realized that their real value proposition wasn't cloud storage or collaboration tools, but reducing transcription errors and speeding up data retrieval. When we reframed the messaging toward this unseen battle, adoption accelerated.

Once all competitive forces are identified, commercial professionals should systematically map how all these competitive forces are positioned.

Here, the two critical questions to be answered are:

1. What are all the attributes that customers value in the category that you will compete in?
2. How much weight does each competitor place on each attribute?

Answering these questions will enable commercial teams to avoid inadvertently positioning offerings similar to others, to stay away from noisy parts of the market, and to capitalize on the gaps.

This analysis can provide data that is easily visualized, as shown in Figure 4-2.

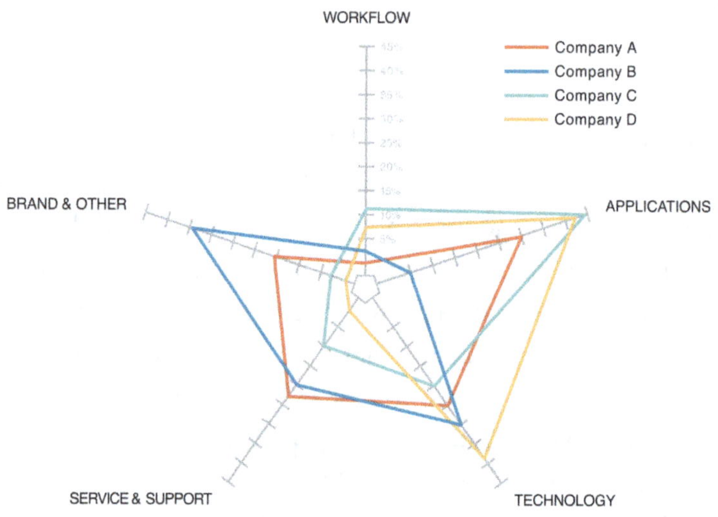

Figure 4-2: Depiction of positioning from four competitive products revealing the differences in each company's positioning. For example, Company D (yellow) positions its product based on technology and applications, whereas Company B (blue) is engaged in leveraging its brand and its technology. No company discusses workflow-related attributes, presenting an opportunity.

A molecular diagnostics testing company we supported had always messaged around "unmatched sensitivity." But after evaluating the competitive landscape and mapping messaging trends, we discovered that all competitors were now claiming similar levels of sensitivity. However, no one addressed the "total time to decision" area including typical time for sample-to-transport to the lab, which is the wait time for sample prep, analysis, reporting and result communication. This client had incremental advantages in each of these steps, which together created a meaningful differentiator. We reframed the brand to emphasize this overlooked but crucial workflow element, which better aligned with emerging customer needs and distinguished them in a crowded field.

In his TEDx talk, strategist Alex Smith shares another way to situate a brand or offering within the competitive landscape: determining how it complements the competitive product set. This exercise proves more difficult because most commercial teams are trained to find and exploit the weakness in the competition, but in this exercise, they are looking for the true, undeniable strengths of the competition and then providing a complement to that strength.

Such an exercise is typically fruitful in a crowded market, where every competitor is covering the waterfront with all the attributes, and the terms of the conversation seem to leave no room for differentiation, or in dynamics where a competitor dominates the market. It may seem impossible to find a complement to universal superlatives such as "innovative" or to beat the highest performance in a particular product attribute. Yet smart commercial strategists can position offerings with alternatives such as:

- Tried and true vs. innovative
- Most trusted vs. highest performance
- Durable vs. feature-rich

Again, the key here is to be honest about the strengths of the competitive offerings, and then to create true complements to those strengths.

Customer Dynamics

Even with strong internal and competitive understanding, no strategy is complete without deep engagement with the prospective customer. In highly technical fields, it is common to overestimate how well we understand our buyers. Technical professionals are often characterized through demographics such as job titles, purchasing authority, or firmographic data (i.e., pharma versus academia or company size). But to influence their decision-making, you must understand their deeper context: motivations, routines, cognitive frames, and emotional triggers.

Off-the-shelf reports from syndicated research firms offer a high-level view of market size, growth rates, and macro trends. But they provide no guidance about the emotional granularity needed to develop an insights-led strategy. Moreover, because these reports are publicly available, they offer no competitive advantage.

Technology Adoption

A great place to begin understanding customer dynamics is to engage with a **technology adoption lifecycle** assessment. The framework was developed in the 1960s by Everett Rogers and posits a standard bell-curve distribution of consumer patterns *(Y-axis represents population, and X-axis represents time).*

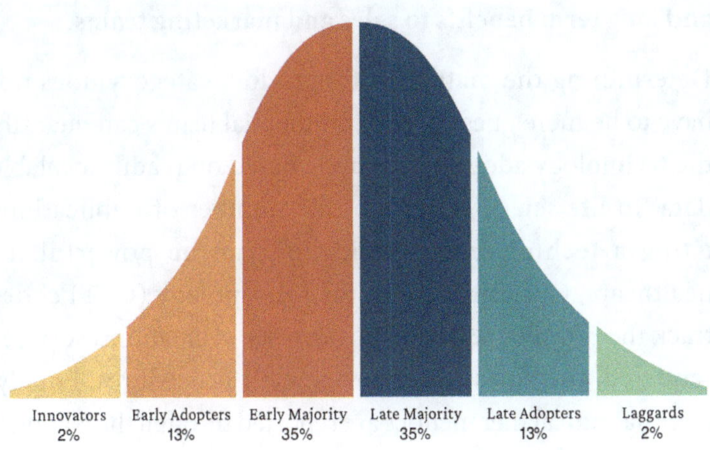

Figure 4-3: The technology adoption life cycle illustrates the relative distribution of any target market based on when they are likely to adopt a new technology that disrupts their current working habits. (Adapted from the Harvard Business Review[1] with adjusted percentages based on my experience)

The curve was popularized by Geoffrey Moore in *Crossing the Chasm: Marketing and Selling Technology Products to Mainstream Consumers*. It helps identify whether the category is in the early adopter phase, early majority phase, or laggard stage. This distinction shapes how companies should approach their audience. Early adopters are excited by novelty and performance; late adopters prefer risk mitigation and easy options.

---

1 Jeremy Korst, "The Technology-Adoption Life Cycle," Harvard Business Review, April 9, 2024, https://hbr.org/data-visuals/2024/03/the-technology-adoption-life-cycle.

The predictable behavior of audiences within each stage of the technology adoption life cycle offers both immediate and long term benefits to sales and marketing teams.

Determining the maturity of a product category does not have to be mere guesswork. Commercial teams can quantify the technology adoption life cycle based on readily available data. In life science research, the number of publications citing a technique or application can be powerful. In healthcare, Current Procedural Terminology (CPT) codes track the prevalence of diagnostic tests, evaluations, services rendered, therapies, and management procedures. Finally, pharmaceutical therapeutics are reported through the National Prescription Audit (NPA) database, which tracks prescription activity in the US.

For example, Figure 4-4 illustrates the maturity of single-cell versus bulk RNA sequencing as of this writing. It is clear in this graph that bulk RNA sequencing was in the late majority stage of the technology adoption life cycle by the end of 2024, whereas single-cell RNA sequencing was entering the early majority phase. While both product categories are in the same market (genomics RNA sequencing), audiences behave very differently toward offerings pertaining to single-cell analysis versus bulk sequencing.

Audiences in every stage of the technology adoption life cycle have needs, and while they may be functionally the same, these needs manifest through very different psychographic lenses. Understanding this frame of reference is one of the most critical variables in achieving high sales velocity.

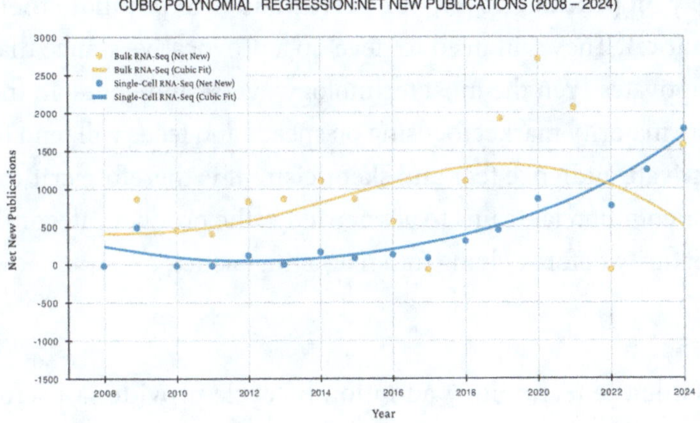

Figure 4-4: A proxy of market adoption for two methods of sequencing, as depicted by the number of net new annual publications, show distinct shapes of each curve, suggesting that bulk RNA sequencing is entering the late majority, while single-cell RNA sequencing is entering the early majority market.

Once the product category's maturity has been defined, commercial teams need to decide whether their offering represents a disruption to the status quo to determine which audience segment to target.

Investigating the technology adoption life cycle provides insight into *how* commercial teams can incite *creativity* in their audience's minds.

Regardless of their psychographic behavior in adopting new technology, every technical professional still embarks on their own buying journey. **As more life science and health technologies enter the late majority phase of the technology adoption life cycle, commercial leaders can no longer simply**

rely on product novelty or performance to populate their market. They will need to develop a provocative stance that captivates even the most technology-averse audiences. In the late majority market focusing on speeds and feeds will tend to activate audience fear and skepticism. It is therefore critical for commercial teams to acknowledge the product category's maturity before delving into marketing tactics.

Qualitative Research

While the technology adoption lifecycle provides a useful proxy for how customers may behave in a given category, nothing is more valuable than **deep, qualitative research**. Unlike surveys, which quantify what is already known, qualitative investigation helps discover what truly matters and how customers will act to different stimuli. Through structured interviews, focus groups, or ethnographies, commercial teams can explore why customers behave the way they do through uncovering tensions, blind spots, and latent needs—the ones buyers aren't consciously aware of until they're named aloud.

Taking the time to examine market dynamics from the audience's own perspective is the single most powerful way of optimizing a commercial strategy for efficacy. This ensures your strategy will drive the target audience to take the actions that will benefit you. Cataloging customer dynamics takes the guesswork out of the equation and hedges against competitive neutralization.

This is not the typical "voice of customer" analysis. Understanding the audience requires a very specific investigation into the market's debates, tensions tradeoffs that audiences face in their work, and how they will react to stimuli when faced with those tradeoffs. Every market category is faced with a debate, and commercial teams would benefit from understanding their audience's psychology in context of such debates.

Let's examine an example of the debates that dominate the conversation in a variety of market segments as of this writing. Back to DNA sequencers: one debate in genomics revolves around the utility of long-read sequencing. In the broader oncology community, there are multiple debates ranging from current cost versus the value of novel precision therapeutics such as cell therapies, as well as how to leverage genomic profiling within the care continuum.

In specific oncological specialties, there are debates about whether and when to stick to standard frontline therapies or whether to leverage subtypes and start with more intensive treatments such as immunotherapies. In infectious disease diagnostics, the debates revolve around the tradeoffs of speed versus efficiency, especially as diagnostics move toward point-of-care. These debates provide landscape contours in which commercial teams can then search for additional nuanced understanding about audiences.

Commercial teams can explore audience perceptions through a variety of research methods. But the most critical factor is objectivity. **Marketing and sales teams must delve into the audience's dynamics independently of the company's agenda, bias, product offerings, or initiatives.** The information gathered should be inherent to the audiences themselves, not biased by retrofitting a need to match the offering's benefit.

Synthesizing to Achieve an Insight

While the action paths should be clear from the results of the analyses described in this chapter, these tools do not necessarily illuminate the strategy itself. Once commercial teams and managers have collected and analyzed the information, the difficult task of synthesis begins. Here, commercial teams need to employ creative thinking to find the optimal path for engaging with the market.

Most business-savvy managers employ deductive reasoning in their daily work, starting from previous experiences and then analyzing a series of cause-and-effect ideas, reasoning every step of the way. The greatest analysts have a finely honed ability to explain complex information and apply reason to make sense of the system being interrogated. But analysis is one thing. Synthesis is something else.

Strategies based solely on deductive reasoning are accessible to any smart analyst privy to the same information and therefore create a transparency risk for the company's plans. In other words, if you have deduced your strategy by reaching the logical conclusion from reading market reports, you can make a fairly safe bet that all of your competitors can guess your strategy, which provides you with no competitive advantage.

Developing a powerful strategy requires synthesis through a critical look, which is fundamentally a creative act. It demands the ability to survey the landscape without overreliance on the past or over-rationalization. Instead, game-changing opportunities generally require commercial teams to take bold leaps beyond the common perspective and venture into associative thought. By allowing yourself to make observations from totally different situations and having the audacity to entertain answers to improbable "what if" questions, you will create the potential for transformative decisions and plans.

Consider the following audacious questions that were once explored by managers in the life science and health industry:

- IDT asked, "What if biologists hate the difficult task of synthesizing their own DNA fragments so much that they'd be willing to buy it as a service?"
- Quartzy asked, "What if we provided a free tool to customers to track their lab inventory, so that we can help them manage and buy the things they need?"
- Covidien dared to question, "What if we don't approach the hospital as a single account, but five different areas of care?"
- Lily Direct asked, "What if a pharma company could sell its therapeutics to patients directly?"

All of these are examples of "what if" questions that led to novel commercial strategies. Bold thinking has completely redefined the landscape and is exactly the type of thinking required to synthesize a strategy based on situation analysis. After collecting the necessary data, you should embrace the opportunity to iterate strategies.

Synthesis alone isn't sufficient for commercial success. The next step in building a powerful commercial strategy is segmentation—the discipline of dividing the market into distinct groups of technical professionals who share common needs, behaviors, and decision-making patterns. Without this foundation, even the most thoughtful and researched commercial efforts will fall flat.

With a solid situation analysis, commercial teams can then identify their product-market fit.

CHAPTER 5

The *Market* Side of the Product Fit: Segmentation

Synopsis

Why do so many companies struggle to find their place in the market, even when their products are genuinely innovative? More often than not, the underlying issue is a poor segmentation strategy. Market segmentation is not a tactical checkbox; it is the structural foundation upon which product-market fit and commercial success are built. This chapter explores why segmentation matters, how to do it properly, and how to evaluate the viability of your chosen segments with a practical framework.

In this chapter, you'll learn how to:

- Understand why segmentation is essential to product-market fit
- Distinguish between demographics and segments
- Use internal data, qualitative insights, and editorial trends to identify potential market segments

- Apply a four-part viability test to evaluate whether a segment is worth targeting
- Avoid common segmentation traps, including overgeneralization and the "ideal client profile" fallacy
- Activate segments in real-world campaigns using dynamic, behavior-driven messaging

You'll come away with a clearer understanding of what makes a segment actionable and valuable and how to stop guessing and start targeting the right market for your product.

Technology Rarely Defines Your Strategy

Over the past two decades, advances in technology have transformed how commercial teams gather data, target audiences, and deliver messages with unprecedented precision. From behavioral tracking to AI-driven personalization, the ability to measure and optimize campaigns in real time has never been greater. Yet, despite these tools, overall effectiveness in reaching and converting technical audiences has not meaningfully improved. This disconnect stems from widespread technophilia: an overreliance on tools that has led many marketing and sales teams to mistake tactical precision for strategic clarity. As a result, the foundational work of segmentation is often neglected, creating the illusion that sophisticated targeting techniques can substitute for a clear understanding of whom the product is truly for.

Technology Rarely Defines Your Market

I once led a positioning exercise for a life science company that made Quantitative Polymerase Chain Reaction (qPCR) instruments. When I asked who their target audience was, the product manager confidently replied, "Molecular biologists. Basically everyone who works with DNA." While the answer was earnest, it reflected a common and costly assumption that breadth equals opportunity.

When we probed further together, we clearly saw that narrowing the focus would mean excluding potential customers, and it would be tempting to fear missing out on potential customers in a broad and diverse market like all molecular biologists. In a competitive space, however, broad targeting weakens engagement. The wider the net, the more vague the message, and the more likely it is to be ignored.

Consider how different the needs of a pharma R&D (research and development) lab are from those of a forensics team. A generic message would amount to something like, "We have a better qPCR system; want to buy one?" and may not resonate with either segment. It fails to speak to the nuanced priorities, constraints, or motivations of anyone in particular. And in today's crowded and competitive markets, that's a critical failure.

In decades past, life science companies could rely on technological novelty or functional superiority to drive demand. Today, even the most advanced products are quickly met with competition. And many new offerings must contend not only with rivals but with well-established legacy methods and workflows. In such conditions, marketers need to differentiate their offerings in a unique and compelling way to attract customers. Therefore, segmentation becomes essential, not as a luxury but as a prerequisite for product-market fit.

To put it simply, segmentation is the "market" side of product-market fit. It is how you take a product's general value proposition and tie it to the specific needs, beliefs, and behaviors of an identifiable group. But effective segmentation goes beyond identifying the largest, fastest growing or most identifiable demographics, sectors, or personas. It requires research, insight, and rigorous validation.

What People Misunderstand About Segmentation

A common pitfall in commercial strategy is the overreliance on demographic labels as stand-ins for true segmentation. It's easy to think that breaking your audience into categories like "academic scientists" or "clinical lab managers" constitutes segmentation. But those identifiers often tell you very little about the audience's behaviors, feelings, intents, or actions.

Demographic-level segmentation is also typically supported with surface-level market research. If a study merely describes job functions, tasks, or purchasing steps and timelines, it may feel informative but lacks the strategic depth needed to guide product-market fit or positioning. Similarly, teams may base segmentation on funding cycles or procurement mechanics, all of which are important operational factors, but not strategic insights.

True segmentation is about identifying meaningful groups that share needs, motivations, and beliefs. It is a strategy for achieving product-market fit, not just a way to organize outreach. That's why every proposed segment should be tested against a simple but powerful four-part viability framework.

But before we test for viability, we need to find viable options in the first place.

The Evolution of Marketing Segmentation

Market segmentation is the strategy of dividing a market into subgroups of people with common needs to predict their behavioral response to stimuli. At its core, segmentation is a research exercise.

Segmentation has a long history, originating with demographic and geographic splits in the mid-20th century and expanding into behavioral and psychographic segmentation in the decades that followed. Today, commercial teams in science and healthcare have access to unprecedented tools such as automation platforms, data lakes, machine learning, and real-time feedback loops.

But the availability of tools doesn't equate to strategic success. Many teams find themselves disappointed with the results of campaigns built on sophisticated technology but weak segmentation. What's missing is the ability to identify meaningful differences in how subgroups experience their problems, perceive solutions, and make decisions.

Segmentation today must serve multiple purposes, simultaneously: informing product development, shaping go-to-market approaches, clarifying product-market fit, and helping organizations prioritize among competing opportunities. That process begins with achieving insights. There are two main steps in developing a strong segmentation strategy.

Step One: Achieving Initial Insights

Commercial teams in healthcare and life science often have the advantage of deep domain knowledge. Many have studied or worked in the same scientific environments as their target customers, giving them an intuitive grasp of the audience. But intuition alone isn't enough and can even misdirect a strategy.

Segmentation begins with observing patterns in behavior, aspiration, experience level, and attitudes toward innovation. Of particular interest are the needs that audiences haven't yet articulated, or as I typically call them, their unseen needs. So if the target audience doesn't see these needs, then how do commercial teams identify them? This process requires analyzing information from three sources.

Editorial trends can offer unexpected clarity. Thought pieces and opinion articles in respected journals often expose rifts, values, or emerging beliefs within a field. Tracking those conversations can reveal not only *what* people care about but *why* and how the information can be used to define meaningful segments. Identifying these discourses helps commercial teams see which side of a debate may benefit them and segment their market more effectively by spotting factions within a general category.

Internal data also plays a role. Sales patterns, web analytics, and engagement rates offer clues about what's working and where interest lies. But numbers must be contextualized. A one-time purchase from a top-tier customer might look like validation, but unless it's repeated and scalable, it's just a data point. For example, it's one thing to have the top 20 pharma companies purchase a single quantity of a novel instrument, because they cannot afford to miss a promising technology. It's another altogether to have them adopt the instrument into their technology stack.

While many healthcare and life science companies have no shortage of information in databases for marketing, sales, support and shipping, the majority of such data remain dark or are unstructured to be of immediate utility. As AI continues to infiltrate every aspect of work, commercial teams and leaders must find ways to leverage their data to guide their strategies and tactics.

Internal data can provide clues and direction about a market, but commercial professionals should take caution and not only rely on such data for strategy. Internal data provides a skewed view, and while it may provide useful observations about the company or offering's experience in the market, such data doesn't substitute for achieving insight or crafting a strategy. Commercial teams should leverage internal data as proverbial traffic signals and signposts on a journey to dominating a market, rather than information that will decide the destination in the first place.

Qualitative research is the most critical method for segmentation. Done properly, it reveals what people truly value, fear, aspire to, or resist. For qualitative studies to deliver maximum value, they must go beyond surface-level questions, such as asking respondents to describe their work or articulating their unmet needs, which provide limited actionability. The goal should not be to catalog unmet needs, but to expose the hidden drivers that shape how people think and behave.

Inspired by Nobel Laureate Albert Szent-Györgyi's quote "Discovery consists of seeing what everyone has seen and thinking what no one has thought," my team and I use a series of tools to moderate qualitative studies and to analyze them beyond the words that respondents provide. As technical professionals tend to communicate factually, we sometimes leverage other stimuli such as banks of images to solicit emotional response, and we also listen to changes in tones of voice and even pitch to detect shifts in emotions.

Such tools open the door to achieving insights and actionable segmentation strategies for our clients.

Once you have obtained actionable insights about segments with common attributes that you believe will provide them with a growth path, you should then test the viability of these segments to determine which one(s) to pursue.

Step Two: Determining Viable Market Segments

Any segmentation strategy should be tested against four basic criteria. In dividing the market into segments, commercial teams can use a simple rubric to evaluate whether their segmentation strategy will serve them well. This viability test requires sales and marketing teams to answer four questions about their potential segments.

First, is the group homogeneous? Do its members share a key attribute or need that makes it likely they'll respond similarly to a tailored message or solution? One of the most common objections I receive in advance of a positioning exercise is the notion that the company has multiple audiences and, therefore, needs multiple positioning strategies. This rarely proves to be the case, because a segment can cut across demographics. For example, an academic scientist and one employed by a pharma company may display different ways of evaluating and purchasing a product, but they may ultimately have the same need and respond predictably to a solution. In this case, they are all part of a single segment.

Second, is the group profitable? This doesn't mean the segment must generate the lion's share of your revenue, but it should offer a return on investment or a strategic advantage worth pursuing.

Third, is the group identifiable? If you can't find and reach the audience, it doesn't matter how valuable they might be. Sometimes you can easily identify and target a segment based on their demographics or *a priori* targeting (e.g., cancer researchers attend a cancer research conference, so you can easily target them at such venues), but other times, you have to segment them *post facto* (e.g., targeting surgeons who suffer from back pain would require targeting all surgeons and providing those with back pain with an opportunity to identify themselves). By contrast, some groups are not easily identifiable (e.g., scientists who are technology laggards).

And finally, **is the segment stable?** Targeting a group based on fleeting interest or temporary shifts in behavior is rarely sustainable. Look for attributes tied to enduring needs or patterns. It would be an unprofitable endeavor to target an audience based on a fleeting market need, but I have seen too many efforts that try to ride an opportunity based on a news cycle (e.g., too many companies rushed into the market with COVID-19 tests well after the demand had stabilized). While a nimble company can capitalize on such movements in the market, such efforts should not be confused with segmentation strategy or product-market fit. Even if the people in a segment change over time (i.e., post-doctoral fellows), the criteria defining the segment should remain consistent.

If the answer to all four of these questions is "yes," then the segment is viable.

Segmentation in Action

Let's consider a scenario common in life sciences: A company wants to shape the market and its segmentation strategy for their webinar funnel. The commercial team has decided to target senior directors in large pharma companies who are in charge of evaluating new technologies. The team prepares a webinar on the burgeoning technique of spatial RNA profiling and collects hundreds of registrants through digital ads and email marketing. The typical playbook might follow with a generic email sequence, leading to low engagement and poor conversion.

But this company's team is far more sophisticated. During the registration process, they asked registrants a simple question: what best describes your interest in this topic? With three well-chosen options, each click becomes a self-reported signal. Now the company can speak differently to researchers pursuing exploratory studies, clinical users validating diagnostics, and technologists who are comparing the latest platforms.

While most teams would likely create a generic set of follow-up messages to generate interest with all of the webinar registrants, this team stays true to their segmentation strategy and creates specific follow-ups to further nurture technologists comparing platforms.

Segmentation in this case doesn't just guide messaging, it improves lead qualification, enriches the data model, and increases the likelihood of conversion down the line. And unlike static personas, it reflects real-time behavior.

The Next Focus

Once a segmentation strategy has passed its viability test, commercial leaders can begin translating those insights into positioning. While many organizations have the tools to target and track, the art and science of knowing what to say to each segment and when to deliver each message can feel daunting. This is where the other side of the product-market fit strategy delivers the key to success: positioning.

With strong segmentation in place, the next step is to develop positioning that makes your value proposition resonate with each segment in a clear, compelling way.

Segmentation allows you to divide the market. Positioning allows you to conquer it.

That's what we'll explore in the next chapter.

CHAPTER 6

The *Product* Side of the Market Fit: The Art & Science of Positioning

Synopsis

The positioning of a product most often determines its success or failure. More art than science, developing a strong positioning strategy requires *practice*. This chapter provides a quick overview of positioning and then presents several guidelines for developing strong positioning strategies. Specifically, we will review the following:

- Definition of positioning
- Elements of a positioning strategy document
- The format for writing a strong positioning statement
- Positioning challenges and pitfalls
- Useful aphorisms for developing positioning strategies

Throughout the chapter, I will offer examples and case studies to better illustrate the concepts of creating a winning positioning strategy.

The Simplification Problem

"We have a really good story to tell to the market. We just don't know how exactly to tell it."

This is the most common phrase I hear when first meeting with our clients. Probing further, they usually describe the difficulty of articulating their value by saying one of two things:

1. "All of our competitors are already using all the same words and the same claims. It seems like we can't cut through the noise," or
2. "Our value/benefits/competitors/differentiators depend on which part of the market we're talking about."

In many cases, they have a great offering with validated performance, but can't succinctly articulate the value.

This is not a matter of simplifying the complex, and it shouldn't "depend" on who you're talking to at that moment. This is a positioning problem.

The instinct of most commercial teams is usually to simplify. But clarity without substance leads to vagueness. And vagueness kills positioning.

Here's an example of how well-intentioned commercial efforts fail to reach their potential:

Several years ago my team and I worked with a company to launch a new line of PCR instruments for research. After years of product development and innovation in user experience, this company had created a truly remarkable line of instruments. Having been inspired by the trend in consumer electronics to optimize intuitive user experience, the commercial team had introduced their new line by touting "simplicity through innovation" to capture that essence. But the message failed to resonate with target audiences, even during beta testing.

Although simplicity was the vision that the company had for this product line, the core problem was not complexity. They had assumed what their audience wanted instead of validating what the market wanted. Their message relied on abstraction ("simplicity through innovation") and an unsubstantiated market need ("scientists want innovation"). But those assumptions didn't hold up under scrutiny.

So we went back to the lab, literally. We first took a walk through the company's own application lab, where a technician gave us a rundown of the new instrument series. As she explained, my team and I couldn't find a single differentiator. To us, it was a standard PCR system with fairly standard workflow features.

Even after conducting interviews with scientists, we discovered that no one was particularly dissatisfied with their current PCR instruments. Functionally, they were just fine. There was no apparent reason to switch.

I was beginning to worry for the client, but when we asked scientists to demonstrate how they use their current PCR systems, we found major tension. The existing systems created daily inefficiencies such as shared machines that required protocols to be reprogrammed on each instrument resulting in frozen software ("the blue screen of death" many researchers called it), failed runs and routine workarounds.

This became our insight. Not a better PCR system. A better way to do PCR. That repositioning transformed how the product was perceived and ultimately led to a significant increase in sales. *Today, this company is one of the market leaders in PCR instrumentation.*

The Definition of Positioning

Positioning is the exact definition of a product's identity. *It explicitly expresses what a product is and implicitly reveals what it is not.* In practice, it identifies the value of a product for a specific group of people who have a common need and differentiates the product from similar offerings.

While developing a strong positioning strategy is often seen as an art, it is one that improves with the right frameworks and deliberate practice. **I use a three-part framework that helps ensure the clarity of the story and encourages robustness of thinking.**

- **A formal positioning statement** is the most rigorous expression of positioning, and is comprised of all relevant information that describes how the offering should be situated in the marketplace.
- **The value proposition** is the central statement that describes the value of an offering for audiences.

- **Core claims to value** are supporting proof points that substantiate the value proposition.

Positioning is typically articulated in a deceptively simple strategy document, consisting of three pieces of information. This document is strictly for internal audiences, meant to align all internal stakeholders around the definition of the product and to create the foundational brief for all communications to come.

As with any framework, one must resist the temptation to reduce the process to merely filling out a form or template and not bypass the substantial thinking required to derive a strong positioning.

The Formal Positioning Statement

The formal positioning is part of an internal strategy document, designed to identify the specific place within the landscape that an offering occupies. It is a single paragraph containing two sentences that describe the offering's worth and differentiation for a defined audience. While several common positioning formats are in practice, I recommend the following format, which was popularized by Geoffrey Moore and which contains six variables highlighted in parentheses:

For (audience)

Who need (a need, independent of the offering),

The (offering name and category) *provides* (benefit).

Unlike (competitive forces), *offering* (is different in a unique way).

Below is an example of the positioning statement for the aforementioned line of PCR thermocyclers:

> *For* scientists in academia and bio-pharma industries routinely using molecular biology methods
>
> *Who need* to make progress in increasingly busy lab environments with shared resources.
>
> *The* new line of PCR instruments *provides* workflow improvements designed specifically for the modern, busy biology lab where scientists need to share resources.
>
> *Unlike* all other PCR instruments, this is the only line of PCR instruments *offering* the ability to port already-programmed protocols from one cycler to the other, remote instrument control and data download access, and plasticware that will never warp during thermocycling.

This positioning format is easy to employ, because it clearly displays all of the variables that require attention. It also ruthlessly sheds light on the vulnerable facets of the offering, necessitating a better understanding of how to develop stronger positioning statements.

I will walk through each of the six variables that make up the formal positioning statement.

The Audience

All audience segments should be listed with as much specific detail as possible, such as:

- By area of specialty

- Job title
- Institution type or demographic
- Regional locations

As a hypothetical example, we can feature biochemists who are primary investigators in North American and European research and discovery labs in pharma companies. The audience information can be even more specific if a product or service is a niche offering.

Audiences are not markets. If managers intend to target biochemists working in the pharmaceutical industry, the audience should be explicitly stated, as in the above example, instead of merely identifying the "pharmaceutical market" as the audience.

The Need

Given the principles of the Insights-Led Model for Commercial Strategy, it should be of little surprise that identifying the need should be central to the positioning statement. The audience's needs are by definition inherent to the audience instead of the product. **In other words, the need should not be reverse-engineered just to justify the product's existence.** Even products that are considered luxuries satisfy a need. The job of sales and marketing teams is to truly understand the need that their offering fills, instead of reverse-engineering a need based on the product's strengths.

For instance, in our investigation of the PCR instrument client's differentiator, we identified that our client had synthesized a need they had not validated: *simplicity*. Our research found the true need: scientists were wasting time and effort habituating to poor workflow design. Our client's product filled that need as soon as it was spotlighted.

In many instances, needs are latent, meaning the audience isn't aware that they have a need. When primed, however, the audience will recognize this need. Marketing and sales efforts based on a deep understanding of the audience's needs will be much more effective than company-centric and self-serving efforts. Technical professionals recognize and reward this effort with their attention and engagement.

The Offering

The offering is not only the description of your product or service, but the chance to define the category in which the offering exists. A novel offering provides an opportunity to define a new category and assume leadership in an unoccupied space in competitive landscapes. However, caution must be taken, as "category design" often proves much more difficult than expected and may require twice as much communications effort to create market acceptance.

The Benefit

The benefit is the product's answer to the audience's needs. While the benefit statement is about the product, it should still be written through the lens of the audience. Benefits are not typically technical specifications or product attributes. Given the technical nature of most life science and healthcare products, benefits may have a technical component. But benefits that resonate with audiences typically transcend specs.

In the PCR example above, the benefit could have focused on fast cycle times or reduced number of incomplete runs (both specs that were true), but the benefit of reduced friction when using the instrument and saving time was the direct answer to the audience's needs.

Competitive Forces

When identifying competitive forces, commercial teams must think beyond direct product competitors to map the complete landscape of how your target audience currently addresses their needs. Mapping the full competitive ecosystem prevents common mistakes such as failing to understand what keeps audiences using familiar but suboptimal products or approaches.

Differentiator

Every offering needs to display at least some facet of uniqueness to justify its existence. With so many parity offerings, products often lack functional differentiators, but differentiators don't necessarily need to be functional in nature; they just need to be demonstrable.

This is an area in which positioning becomes less science and more art, because commercial teams can actually leverage attributes such as product packaging, delivery mechanism, service, support, business model, or new audience segments as a way to achieve differentiation.

In our PCR case, second-round interviews revealed scientists' frustration with poor workflow design, making it clear our client's line of instruments offered a distinct advantage, which we used to claim an unoccupied market position.

Price is usually an unfavorable differentiator, unless the company's manufacturing or service offering has a significant advantage to defend competitive price reductions by a wide margin.

Value Proposition

The value proposition is a concise expression of your product's unique value to a specific audience. A simple structure might be:

- *We are the only [X] that solves [Y] in a unique [Z] way.*

For the line of PCR instruments, the team developed the following value proposition:

> We provide the only line of PCR systems that, through intuitive and integrated user experience enhancements, eliminates the time-wasting workarounds scientists have habituated around.

The term "value proposition" of course includes the word "value." Any formula should address the value in a way that resonates with audiences. The Y problem should refer to some value that the offering provides better than competitive options.

In the Insights-Led Model for Commercial Strategy, the value proposition should guide the audience to form a hypothesis for themselves about how to satisfy their need. Therefore, the

Education stimuli should create an environment for scientists to experience the value proposition.

Core Claims to Value

Every claim must be backed by evidence. While this is obvious in regulated healthcare industries such as therapeutics and diagnostics, non-regulated industries sometimes forget this critical fact, and the result is industry parlance riddled with hyperbole and "marketing speak" that fails to make any impact.

Core claims to value are the supporting proof points that validate your value proposition. They are not raw specs, but explanations, connecting product features to audience benefit.

Recall that the final step in a technical professional's buying journey is to validate their own hypothesis, and that Persuasion stimuli should be designed to provide sufficient demonstration that the solution being offered will fulfill the audience's need.

While there is no specific formula for writing core claims to value, a helpful starting point is to scan for adjectives in the value proposition and provide supporting information to justify such qualifiers. Core claim statements should translate the product's specifications and the benefits stated in the positioning and value proposition.

For the PCR example, the core claims to value included statements that justified the adjectives "time-wasting," "intuitive," and "integrated:"

- Protocols can be shared seamlessly across multiple PCR machines in the lab, eliminating the need to reprogram when your preferred machine is occupied.
- Built-in Wi-Fi and USB connectivity allows direct data transfer for analysis, removing the dependency on printouts and manual data entry.
- Enhanced thermal block design and reinforced sample trays prevent common failures that require protocol restarts and sample reprocessing.
- Patented polymer-based plasticware reinforces 96-well plates in all dimensions, eliminating the danger of warping during runs.

Common Positioning Challenges and Pitfalls

In healthcare and life science, the positioning strategy often fails to drive the intended results. In my experience, one or several common reasons contribute to a weak positioning strategy:

An Overabundant Use of Positioning Attributes

The most straightforward positioning attributes have already been used by competitive companies. Attributes include, but are not limited to:

- Fast
- Easy-to-use
- Inexpensive
- Innovative
- Reliable
- High-quality (my most despised)

Any combination of the above have been used so exhaustively that they have lost their meaning to audiences. In fact, in our research we have documented that technical professionals often take the exact opposite meaning from such facile claims. For example, a group of neuroscientists often cited that when they see "easy-to-use imaging software" they either think the software is actually difficult to use or junk.

In virtually every category, several products and services claim these facile attributes. A useful exercise for transcending easy positioning attributes and developing meaningful positioning strategies is to employ competitive framing: the process of mapping all competitors against two meaningful attributes for a product category in a way that truthfully presents your offering as the clear winner. Recall from situation analysis tools, within any given product category, there will be only a handful of attributes meaningful to the audience. Attributes often need to be redefined or recategorized to frame the product as the most compelling choice. (See Figure 6-1.)

The goal of competitive framing is to redefine how the market landscape is viewed. The process typically requires an iterative approach to identify the optimal attributes for mapping the landscape. In employing this tool, you should map attributes against one another and then explore the four narratives that each quadrant represents. Continue this process until a narrative describes a world in which your offering is a clear winner and other narratives in other quadrants describe other competitors.

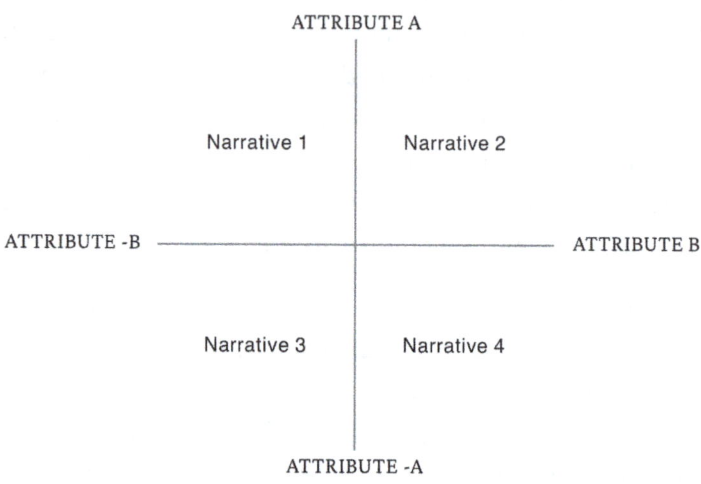

Figure 6-1: Competitive framing involves mapping all competitors against the two most important for prominent attributes for the product category. For example, if sensitivity is on the X-axis, then Attribute B would be high sensitivity and Attribute -B would be low sensitivity.

Overly Complex Positioning

Life science and healthcare companies cater to a highly educated clientele who are well-versed in technical specifics. However, it does commercial professionals no good to confuse education with psychology. Even though a scientist or a doctor has technical needs, their actions still display their human motivations. The audience needs to be sufficiently motivated to plod through the technical complexities of an offering. Even then, they may fail to distill the value proposition for themselves. Although some life science products are technically complex, sales and marketing teams need to distill the main benefits of their offering through the audience's perspective in order to minimize mental roadblocks for them and resolve a psychological tension to create a positive motivation for them to act.

Reactive Positioning Developed due to Competitive Pressures

Most offerings in healthcare and life science face competition, and it feels like human nature for commercial teams to defend their positioning by reacting to competitive claims. Unfortunately this well-intentioned effort usually results in depositioning yourself, which usually does not win the battle for market leadership.

The true battle is not against competitors, but against the dynamics of successfully navigating an offering through the adoption life cycle. This shift in mindset will naturally change the market, forcing other competitors into rearguard action.

As Henry Ford aptly said, "The competitor to be feared is one who never bothers about you at all, but goes on making his own business better all the time." **Be that competitor.**

An Overfocus on Delivery Instead of Strategy

In my experience, too many healthcare and life science companies spend lots of resources in creating content and/ or adopting the latest digital marketing tools that promise precision strikes on target audiences, all without a strong positioning strategy.

No matter how creative the marketing materials are or if they're delivered through the latest tech stack, **if the message does not appropriately position the offering in a way that**

drives an urgent flutter in the hearts of your audience, the marketing program will fail to result in successful sales. It will be useless noise.

Without a doubt, the creative execution of any commercial effort is critical in grabbing attention and establishing attributes in the minds of the intended audience. But if the strategy is faulty or pedestrian, even the most creative of campaigns will fail to persuade technical audiences. True creativity starts with applying talent to a strong positioning strategy, not to clever advertisements or marketing headlines.

Testing the Strength of Positioning Strategies

Strong positioning is best built through a systematic approach that combines industry knowledge, a secret about the market, strategic savvy, and bold thinking. Given the likelihood of going astray at least once during a positioning exercise, I recommend applying a five-question test to determine whether your positioning strategy is strong.

1. **Does it Cut the Market Like a Knife?**

   Development of an exact definition of the product requires a positioning strategy that will sharply segment the market. **A strong positioning severs the market into two clearly distinguished groups: one that comprises your potential customers and one that represents the rest of the world.**

   The entire market is not–and can't be–"your market." The purpose of positioning is to determine which segment of the market the offering can enter and quickly dominate and in which it will have an absolute advantage. Sharp positioning will create the focus needed within the commercial team to focus on the prize. The focused commercial team can ignore all other possible markets, no matter how tempting.

This adage has tremendous implications, because it relieves the need to cram every positive attribute of a product into a positioning statement to avoid leaving anything out in fear of losing a potential customer.

2. Does It Tell the Truth?

Good positioning absolutely requires that commercial teams tell the truth. Marketing and sales messages are distillations of truths designed to reach specific audiences, not deceive them.

On occasion, I have heard sales and marketing executives claim that they have permission to color the truth. This is commercial malpractice. Embellishments that arise in a positioning strategy might rarely come from outright dishonesty. They are more likely the result of an especially challenging market dynamic or an offering with challenging attributes or little differentiators. Instead of resorting to coloring the truth, commercial strategists should work harder to solve the challenge. In fact, a parity product presents an opportunity for commercial strategy's finest hour. (Remember, if table salt can be differentiated, so can your product. You can do this!) Smart strategists will take advantage of such opportunities to shine.

Equally important, failure to tell the truth makes the Insights-Led Model for Commercial Strategy utterly ineffective. False statements will only desensitize the audience in the end, and at some point in the technical professionals' buying journeys, the truth will manifest, sending all subsequent efforts straight into the technical professional's filter—forever.

Lying on a positioning statement is lying to yourself.

3. Does it Avoid Hyperbole?

This is a refinement of the mandate to tell the truth. The positioning strategy is strictly an internal document, meant to align all of the stakeholders. It is neither brochure copy nor ad headline, although it will eventually guide the development of campaigns and sales pitches. It serves no purpose to exaggerate, because internal embellishment is transparent and purposeless. An adorned positioning statement is a classic symptom of some internally perceived weakness in the offering, in which case commercial teams feel it is necessary to resort to hyperbole. This is where creative thinking and hard work pay off when applied to achieving a strong positioning. Hyperbole simply does not possess such thrust.

4. Does it Retrofit the Audience Needs?

This is perhaps the most crucial question in the test for a strong, artful positioning strategy. Sales and marketing teams must take care never to reverse-engineer the audience needs to fit the product's attributes.

For example, a mass spectrometer with truly superb resolution does not translate into the positioning statement that starts with, "For researchers who need higher resolution." The true audience need is always completely independent of any company or offering, and in this example, researchers use resolution as a means to some other end. Shrewd strategists focus on finding the true need.

5. **Does it Focus on a Single Benefit?**

Positioning statements require commercial sales and marketing teams to identify a precise benefit for a specific audience. But what if one's product offers multiple benefits that seem equally compelling? Such a conundrum is often solved in one of two ways.

You can either make a tough decision and choose the single benefit that best answers the audience's need or put effort into synthesizing the multiple benefits into a single, meaningful benefit statement that addresses the audience's need.

Diagnosis of Weak Positioning Statements

To practice, each of these three positioning statements possesses a critical flaw, which can be diagnosed by applying the five-question test. I offer these so you can determine how to spot the weakness in positioning strategies in your own work:

Example 1:

For scientists in proteomics biomarker discovery in academic laboratories worldwide,

Who need to automate their workflows,

The XX liquid-handling system provides a validated workflow for automation of biological samples for biomarker discovery.

Unlike other automation systems that offer only general tools for automation, the XX liquid-handling system has been preconfigured specifically for biomarker analysis.

Here, the audience need is retrofitted to what the liquid-handling system provides. Automating workflows is technical and dependent on the particularities of any platform—it is not independent of the offering. The need behind automated workflows might instead be to save time, be more productive, reduce costs, maximize data collection in experiments using precious biological samples, or reduce sample-to- sample variability. The need is not automation.

Example 2:

For laboratory managers across all of life sciences,

Who need to maintain a healthy working environment for the laboratory,

The XX Pipette system provides a proven reduction in ergonomic stress for its operators.

Unlike other pipette suppliers, the XX Pipette system has been dedicated to its customers with a 50-year history.

This statement lacks a meaningful differentiator. To state that a pipette system is "dedicated to its customers with a 50-year history" is hyperbolic brochure-speak.

This differentiator statement lacks a precise reference to anything that will resonate with audiences regarding their needs. It is true that handheld pipettes are ubiquitous tools and offer little in functional differentiation. Such situations call for more creative and honest strategy.

There is a potential differentiator hidden in the "proven ergonomic benefit" that could be especially useful to a subsegment of laboratory workers. If the company opted to pursue such market segmentation, I might advise them to focus on specific workflows involving rapid, high-volume pipetting needs.

Example 3:

> For directors of food and consumer safety testing laboratories
>
> Who need absolute assurance in the validity of their results,
>
> The XX ICP-MS elemental analysis system provides sensitivity down to one part per trillion.
>
> Unlike other ICP-MS providers, the XX ICP-MS system is upgradable to tandem MS-MS detection for additional sensitivity.

Here, the supposed benefit is merely a technical specification. Sensitivity down to one part per trillion does not create a human experience of a met need. But this sensitivity enables the audience to achieve better methods to ensure consumer safety. A more resonant benefits statement would focus on such possibilities.

Leveraging Positioning in a Digital World

Today, the sheer volume of sales and marketing solicitation is everywhere: from personal communications tools like phone and email to the environment and everything in between. We are bombarded with material that may be relevant to our needs but we are not willing to interact with. As a result, trust has become a form of currency, and one that is rapidly degrading.

In healthcare and life science, relationships are everything. While technology can help create, magnify, and maintain relationships, no technology to date has been able to fill the void created by a shallow or flawed positioning strategy. The fundamentals of strong positioning have not changed.

Although developing a strong positioning strategy is hard, it remains one of the most essential aspects of commercializing an offering and should be treated with the necessary rigor and creativity to be powerful and actionable. Segmentation is half of the product-market fit, and great positioning is the other half.

Once the positioning strategy is approved, commercial teams need to translate the strategy into a road map that maximizes results.

How to Win the Game With Psychology

CHAPTER 7

Engineering for Action: Creating an Action-Inducing Commercial Plan

Synopsis

Commercial strategy is the integrated engine of market success, encompassing what has traditionally been split into "sales" and "marketing," but functioning as one unified system. Its purpose is to deliver revenue. Every activity, from initial audience engagement to the close of a sale, exists to capture the reasonable share of the market within a defined time frame. There are many performance indicators along the way, but these are diagnostics, not endpoints. If the strategy is strong and executed well, revenues will reflect it. If revenues fall short, the strategy has failed. No other metric matters.

This chapter explores how to design and execute commercial strategy as an end-to-end system built to generate revenue. It examines how to set unified objectives, map the modern buyer's journey, apply behavioral science to create experiences that move prospects, anticipate and remove buying barriers, and orchestrate **Leadership, Education, and Persuasion stimuli** that lead to measurable market capture.

In this chapter, we will discuss:

- Why revenue is the single, definitive measure of commercial success
- How to use indicators at each stage without replacing the central metric
- Mapping and adapting to the modern, non-linear buying journey
- Applying behavioral science principles to create memorable buyer experiences
- Building a Leadership, Education, and Persuasion messaging roadmap that drives market share growth

A Metric for Commercial Strategy: Aligning on the Right Objective

In many organizations, sales and marketing still operate on different scorecards. Marketing is often judged on leads, opportunities, engagement rates, or impressions; sales is measured on deals closed and sales cycle times. This separation fosters misaligned priorities and undermines the reality that both functions are part of the same commercial enterprise.

A true commercial strategy has a single, non-negotiable measure of success: **revenue generated within the defined market opportunity**. Everything else—website traffic, leads, social engagement, event attendance, sales velocity, even sales pipeline—is an **indicator**, not an outcome. Indicators matter because they reveal the health of each stage in the system, but they should never be confused with the goal itself.

If the commercial strategy is well-conceived and executed, revenues will reflect it. If revenues fall short, the strategy has failed, regardless of whether interim indicators looked promising. A campaign may generate high engagement, but if it fails to create and close real opportunities, it is not successful. Conversely, a campaign with modest engagement metrics but strong conversion into paying customers can be highly effective.

When sales and marketing share the same ultimate metric, accountability is unified. The conversation shifts from defending functional outputs to diagnosing the commercial system's performance end-to-end. Indicators such as awareness levels, number of opportunities entering the pipeline, or progression rates between buying stages are used diagnostically to identify where the strategy is breaking down, not as a replacement for the revenue measure.

The Big Misunderstanding

Most companies spend money on a variety of insurance policies. What is the ROI of this money spent, especially since the intention is to never have to invoke such policies?

Why do we actually need sales *and* marketing? If revenue generation is the goal, then is marketing merely sales support? Writing? Sending emails? Putting on tradeshow exhibits? Making pretty graphics? I bet you have already guessed the answer, although I will break it down even further.

Indeed, many life science and healthcare companies starve marketing in favor of sales, due to marketing's lack of "results" and overinflated expectations of the sales department.

Let us explore the axiom that most of the target audience at any one time is not actively on the market for whatever the company is offering. To break this down further, we can safely assume that any moment in time:

- 75% of a market is not even aware that they have a need
- 20% is aware of a need but aren't actively looking for a solution
- 5% is actively in the market

So, what is the role of sales and marketing in this dynamic?

A savvy marketing department has three roles:

1. To invite the 75% of the unaware market to **recognize that they have a need**
2. To engage with the 20% of the inactive aware market to **shape the way they should evaluate a solution**
3. To **engender trust** with the 5% active buyers in the market

The sales team's job is to ensure revenues are realized *today*, and marketing's job is to support this endeavor, but more importantly to ensure revenues are realized *tomorrow*. In many ways, marketing is the insurance policy that a company takes out on its future revenue pipeline.

I hope my explanation above will inspire commercial teams to align on the ultimate goal of their organization and to provide the needed authority to both their sales and marketing teams to do their respective jobs toward that ultimate goal. Now, let us turn our attention back to the most important actor in any company's story: the customer and their journey.

Mapping the Modern Customer Journey

The traditional Awareness/Interest/Desire/Action (AIDA) model and the linear funnel were once adequate approximations of buyer behavior. Today, they are relics. Given the overabundance of channels that a typical consumer is exposed to every hour of every day, buyers operate in a non-linear, dynamic environment. In healthcare and life science, typical buyers may encounter a brand through an article, drop away for months, see a peer reference on LinkedIn, attend a webinar, then revisit the company's website, search the literature, talk to additional colleagues, return to the company's website, and be exposed to the company's presence at a tradeshow before engaging in a substantive conversation with a company's representative.

A better analogy to a linear funnel is a three-dimensional cone, where prospects enter from multiple points, move in and out at different levels, and interact with a variety of touchpoints before making a decision. This dynamic journey requires commercial strategies to **engineer experiences**—deliberate, memorable encounters that make the value proposition tangible.

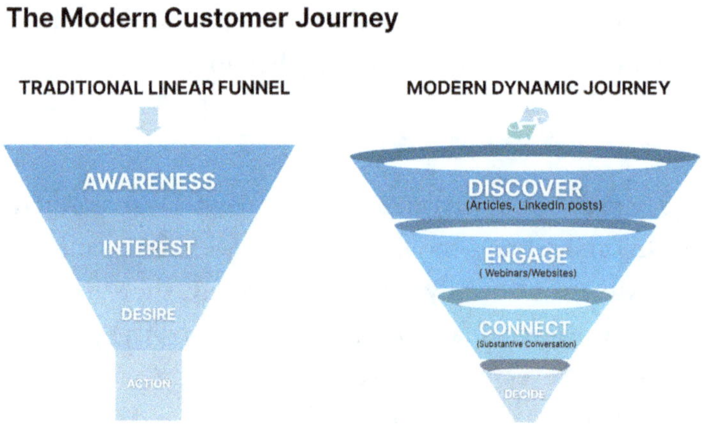

The Modern Customer Journey

Figure 7-1: The evolution of the "funnel" to a modern customer journey, represented in a three-dimensional cone. Customers get input from a vast array of sources during their decision journey. They can move up or down the cone based on their interaction and the influence that stimuli has on them.

Sensory and emotional cues can be powerful. Just as Netflix's sonic logo or a computer's startup chime instantly trigger recognition, a well-crafted B2B experience can create lasting mental association.

The Charles River Laboratories story from Chapter 1 illustrates this: by pairing a real patient with the scientists who helped her and staging a private concert with Ginger, the company created an emotional moment that transcended conventional messaging. The short film produced from this event generated over 12 million impressions and over 2 million complete views in the first 6 weeks, but more importantly, it deepened trust and affinity, laying groundwork for commercial relationships that translated into revenue. I have personally seen the film over 100 times, and I still get choked up every time.

Modern commercial strategies must embrace the reality: buyers are no longer progressing step-by-step down a linear funnel; they are navigating a web of touchpoints, distractions, and competing messages. The challenge is not to force linearity, but to keep them engaged inside the cone until they are ready to commit.

The most effective way to engage audiences in this new reality is to orchestrate memorable experiences, engineered to transmit a specific psychological message.

Behavioral Science Tools for Memorable Experiences

(The following passage is my experience with using principles described by Robert Cialdini's work)

Commercial professionals often underestimate the role of human psychology in technical buying. While decisions in life sciences and other technical sectors require data and logic, the pathways to attention, trust, and preference are shaped by the same cognitive biases and heuristics that govern consumer behavior.

Engaging the senses creates a type of information transfer called **somatic learning** and results in deeper retention and emotional connection. A lab tour, an interactive demonstration, or a narrative video featuring relatable peers can engage visual, auditory, and emotional channels simultaneously.

Several well-established behavioral science principles are particularly relevant and very useful in creating memorable experiences in technical markets. I provide them as inspiration for commercial teams to determine how to engage their customers through marketing and sales.

Authority

The brain uses heuristics—or shortcuts—to make decisions. One of these shortcuts is our brain's desire to watch for signals of authority to shape our decisions. Research shows that our brains react to signals of authority no matter who or where they come from.

This behavioral shortcut is the reason why companies with a strong, provocative point of view, those who articulate a powerful Leadership message, usually attract audiences and customers.

Likeness

People respond more favorably to those they perceive as similar to themselves. Highlighting shared professional challenges or values builds rapport. In sales and marketing, connecting over similar interests, values, or experiences builds rapport, signals likeness, and prime audiences to say *yes* more often to the brand or sales rep whom they deem to be like themselves. Likeness is the reason why relationship building is so successful in sales.

Consistency

Why do people tend to sit in the same chair in a conference room or order the same meal from the same restaurant? Once a prospect has taken an action such as attending a webinar, requesting information, or making a specific purchase, reminding them of it increases the likelihood that they will make the same decision, even if it's a bigger purchase or action. This is because people dislike cognitive dissonance and prefer routine.

Invoking the audience's desire for consistency can be very powerful in creating memorable experiences and taking the intended action.

At LINUS, we leverage consistency often to remind people of a prior action. For example, we worked with a life science company who needed to generate live opportunities from a recent lead generation campaign. Only 1% of leads who had requested to hear from the company replied to the sales representative. So, we reframed the email and reminded them of their prior action of requesting a call. The result? **Leads became over 38 times more likely to respond.** Invoking someone's desire for staying consistent with their prior actions can deliver significant, material advantage.

Availability

The availability of an instance of something happening, such as a natural disaster, shapes how humans act, even technically trained professionals. The brain is constantly looking for available instances to connect the dots and sometimes overestimates the frequency with which a situation occurs when an example of the situation comes to mind.

Every commercial team in healthcare and life science looks to address unmet needs for their respective markets. Sometimes, those needs are infrequent and audiences don't feel them as high priority. But an available example can change that. When my team and I were conducting our research for our client selling a line of PCR instruments and plasticware, we encountered this powerful phenomenon. If we asked respondents how often they experienced their plastics warping in the thermocycler, the answer was "not very often at all." But when we asked them to tell us a story of when their plastic plate warped, we watched respondents become animated and visibly agitated as they relived the loss of months of work.

We knew then that we had been asking the wrong question. Asking people how often something happens requires people to become statistical, and they divorce themselves from the actual event or its outcome. But asking them to recount a story makes the feelings associated with that story available to their senses.

Scarcity

People naturally desire what they can't have. Authentic scarcity drives urgency. Artificial scarcity erodes trust, but legitimate constraints such as limited pilot slots and exclusive access can accelerate decisions, even changing perceptions altogether.

I once advised a university to leverage scarcity to successfully change the perception of a new, auxiliary science campus. Initially all of the faculty had declined to move to the new building, for fear of feeling left out of the main innovation that was happening on the main campus. By flipping the script, the administrators created scarcity by reiterating that the new center was state of the art, with all of the latest scientific technologies, and mandated that faculty had to apply for a chance to participate in this new hub. As a result of this seemingly small change, they had 100% occupancy of the new facility within one academic year.

Reciprocity

Reciprocity is an ancient but powerful social norm practiced by all societies in the world. When employed correctly, it's irresistible.

This heuristic drives people to constantly assess and repay debts of all kinds, even small ones. While the feeling of "owing" someone is a strong driver of action, many times people are unaware of their sense of indebtedness. Performing an act of service or providing value *before* asking for something builds goodwill and a sense of obligation.

I know a sales person who immediately looks for something small that needs to be cleaned or tidied up as she enters her prospect's facility and cleans up before starting her sales call. Even such a subtle act creates a reciprocity imbalance.

Consensus

Consensus, or social proof, is the most well-known persuasive technique: People look to the actions of others who are like them to influence their own decisions.

Providing social proof is the most common and effective use of invoking a sense of consensus. Evidence of peer adoption provides reassurance. Specific, relevant examples such as "used by five of the top ten pharma companies" are more compelling than vague claims.

There are many other psychological persuasive techniques that teams can leverage to orchestrate a memorable experience and communicate the brand's value proposition without resorting to words. When applied thoughtfully, these principles help clear the obstacles that slow or prevent technical professionals from advancing in their commercial journey.

Identifying Barriers in the Technical Professionals' Buying Journey

Technical professionals may encounter barriers in each phase of the buying journey. For example:

- In the **Recognition** phase, the buyer may not be aware of the need, may not prioritize it highly enough to take action, or may not connect their need to your offering.
- In the **Exploration** phase, the buyer may have misconceptions, base their hypothesis on erroneous sources, encounter logistical challenges, question the credibility of the company, or have an affinity to a competitive brand.
- In the **Evaluation** phase, the buyer may struggle to validate claims, secure internal approval, or experience the offering in a meaningful way.

A comprehensive situation analysis, including SWOT, often reveals these barriers. Weaknesses and threats in the analysis often translate directly into obstacles that must be removed for progress to continue.

Commercial teams should identify and prioritize the barriers that buyers may face in their decision journey and quantify the impact of each barrier on revenue potential.

A company unknown in a market, for example, faces an awareness barrier that must be addressed before technical professionals will feel enough trust to engage with its Evaluation-stage Persuasion message. In this case, the company's commercial efforts need to prioritize investment toward increasing trust. This is usually achieved through a balance of media exposure (advertising, PR, conference sponsorships) and the provocativeness of the Leadership messaging strategy.

There are additional barriers that sales and marketing teams need to consider, as illustrated in Figure 7-2. For example, the company may be known to audiences for a different type of offering than the one being presented now, or audiences may demand live product demonstrations of a product that is impractical or unfeasible to transport. Listing the most pertinent barriers will guide commercial teams to specific action steps.

The conclusions that are drawn about the potential barriers and their relative importance will elucidate the best tactic to employ to overcome each barrier. Once all barriers are identified, teams must prioritize them and apply resources, content, and tactics appropriately.

Phase	Recognition	Expectation	Evaluation
Barriers	Brand Awareness	Scientific Credibility	Scientific Credibility
	Budgets	Need for Peer Validation	Sales Team Coverage
	Ability to Reach Audience	Lack Reference Customers	Demo Viability
	High Competitive Noise	Commodity Status	Demonstrate Service
	Product Novelty		

Figure 7-2: Typical barriers that may impede scientists as they embark on their buying journey are not limited to the product's weaknesses or competitive threats.

Creating the Stimuli Road Map

In the Insights-Led Model for Commercial Strategy, channel selection, creative conceptualization and content development all come after message development. The **Leadership, Education, and Persuasion Framework** is the structural backbone of persuading technical audiences through their buyer journey.

Leadership Stimuli

Bold and relevant, Leadership stimuli need to challenge assumptions, frame debates, and capture attention. The Leadership message is the gateway that will lead audiences to believe a company's value proposition and is designed to provoke curiosity without alienating potential buyers.

The most well-known example of Leadership messaging is Apple's famous introduction of the Think Different campaign. From the first words "Here's to the crazy ones…" until the last, this campaign reframed the world in the minds of its audiences.

The explosion of media noise makes Leadership messaging a non-negotiable part of the Insights-Led Model for Commercial Strategy. Without a strong, resonant provocation, companies will rarely capture attention and captivate hearts, just as Apple had failed to do for decades with its product-centric value proposition.

Although commercial teams typically display some initial nervousness in committing to a provocation, Leadership messaging is often the most energizing to develop. It calls for creativity and boldness, cutting through market noise with a thought-provoking stance that speaks directly to an audience's core need. Through a solid situation analysis and product-market fit exercise, commercial teams should already understand the major debates within the target segment, making it easier to choose topics that will gain attention. To be effective, however, every Leadership message must also align with the offering's positioning.

Two guiding questions shape strong Leadership messaging:

First, what will command the audience's attention?

In the competitive, distraction-filled healthcare and life science sectors, Leadership messaging must rise above the 1% awareness levels typical of traditional tactics (low bar, I know). Bold, well-reasoned ideas can capture the attention of entire audience segments, but boldness must be balanced with responsibility. Messages should provoke thought, not spike an emotion for its own sake. Irrelevance or offense damages credibility, and in a trust economy, credibility is indispensable.

Second, what action or interaction will this messaging inspire?

A strong Leadership message will naturally resonate with some and not others. This selective appeal is actually an asset as it allows commercial teams to focus on audience segments that are philosophically aligned and most likely to convert. The goal is to engineer an experience for these receptive audiences that sparks curiosity and leads them to seek more information. Leadership messaging typically represents 10–15% of the total content in an insights-led commercial strategy, but it must be crafted to drive the next step in engagement.

Generic calls to action like "Learn more" rarely work. Instead, Leadership messaging should be so compelling that technical professionals feel drawn to follow the path set before them.

Answering these two questions not only refines the Leadership message but also ensures it integrates seamlessly into the broader campaign architecture.

Education Stimuli

Objective, evidence-based, and generous with guiding insight, Education stimuli enable technical professionals to form a hypothesis consistent with the value proposition the company intends for its offering. Education messaging usually dictates the volume and depth of an overall content roadmap and typically maps with nurturing the market's audience. But it is difficult to execute correctly.

Healthcare and life science commercial content plans are usually teeming with attempts to educate their markets, usually through webinars. While labeled educational content, these attempts are usually thinly veiled product demonstrations or passive education that does not drive urgency or intent. The vast majority of these attempts do not support a provocation because the company does not have a Leadership message.

To succeed, every Education stimulus needs to provide evidence for why the Leadership message is real and applicable to the audience, and lead them to form a hypothesis about what they should do as a result of this new frame of reference about their work. Otherwise, such stimulus may capture leads who have no intention of ever purchasing. Too many Customer Relationship Management (CRM) systems in too many healthcare life science companies are filled with these people.

A strong Education strategy answers three guiding questions:

1. What will lead the audience to conclude the value proposition?

The most effective Education messaging delivers consistent, credible proof that the provocation is real and applicable. For example, in positioning the PCR line of instruments, uncovering a hidden problem such as workflow inefficiency required every instance of the Education message to demonstrate how inefficient the workflows were at the time and how much waste was generated as a result. While repetition can feel mundane to the commercial team, it is essential for the audience; without it, the offering risks fading into the noise of undifferentiated products.

2. How will this messaging be turned into content?

Many healthcare and life science organizations face a scarcity of high-quality Education stimuli because of how resource-intensive they are to generate. Since Education messaging often determines the campaign's overall effectiveness, quality must be prioritized.

3. How can this information be repurposed over time?

Education content should not be seen as a one-off exercise; it should feed an ongoing dialogue that nurtures prospects toward taking action. By designing messages that can be reused in different formats, commercial teams can sustain engagement and keep technical professionals moving toward evaluation.

In the modern three-dimensional cone, each touchpoint must be compelling enough to draw the audience deeper into the journey, where Persuasion messaging can complete the case for adoption.

Persuasion Stimuli

Proof-driven and experiential, Persuasion stimuli simulate the experience of becoming a customer, reduce perceived risk, and reinforce the decision to buy by validating the hypothesis about how to satisfy the need or opportunity stated by the Leadership message.

Persuasion messaging is most relevant when technical buyers are actively evaluating options. In an ideal world, they have already encountered provocative Leadership messaging and deep Educational messaging that has framed the way they think about their problem and how to solve it, and the persuasion stage simply confirms what they now believe. In reality, today's three-dimensional buying journey means audiences may encounter persuasion experiences first, last, or several times in between—and each encounter must still move them closer to becoming a customer.

Persuasion messaging works best when it goes beyond sloganeering and moves into showing by immersing technical buyers in the offering's value proposition so they can "try on" what it would be like to be a customer. The goal is to lower evaluation barriers through direct or indirect experiences that make the decision feel inevitable:

1. Which content can offer direct simulation?

The strongest persuasion comes from opportunities to engage directly with the company: pilot programs, in-lab demonstrations, interactive trials, technical workshops, or peer-to-peer reference calls. These experiences not only validate claims but also create mental rehearsal, where buyers can visualize themselves benefiting from the product or service. As one technical professional told me, "I mentally rehearse what it's like to be a customer of the company as I'm evaluating a product."

2. How can indirect immersion be leveraged?

Not all persuasion has to be direct or hands-on. Brand perception, visual identity, tone of communication, campaign design, and even the demeanor of sales teams shape how buyers imagine the customer experience. The Charles River Laboratories campaign is a case in point: By connecting scientists and patients in emotionally charged storytelling, the brand reframed itself as a partner in outcomes, not just a provider of services. This emotional anchor kept prospects engaged and accelerated their movement toward adoption.

3. Which experience can instigate conversations?

Since 2020, remote engagement and "Zoom fatigue" have transformed buyer expectations. Automation and templated outreach are quickly recognized and dismissed, and they are overstuffing inboxes, message apps, and voicemail. Persuasion messaging today thrives in authentic, real-time conversations that invite questions, reveal responsiveness, and leave a lasting human impression.

4. What does the sales team need for experiential selling?

The sales team represents a critical delivery channel for persuasion experiences. That means collaborating with them early to understand the tools such as demos, interactive models, or scenario-based presentations will help them most. Creating these tools in isolation and then "training" sales to use them almost guarantees low adoption. When sales has a hand in designing them, the tools become natural extensions of their conversations.

Persuasion messaging, when engineered as experience rather than information, can meet technical professionals wherever they are in their buying journey, draw them deeper into the cone, and convert consideration into committed revenue.

Each strategy serves a distinct purpose, but all three work toward the single outcome of revenue capture.

Deconstructing Yesterday's Playbook

Automation and AI can extend reach and efficiency, but they are not replacements for strategies. Innovation in commercial strategy comes from insight generation, purposeful engagement, and building trust through repeated value delivery.

One of the most powerful outcomes of the Insights-Led Model for Commercial Strategy approach is the development of **parasocial relationships**, where technical professionals feel a sense of familiarity and trust toward the brand, akin to the rapport with a trusted colleague or mentor. These relationships increase loyalty, shorten sales cycles, and elevate the brand above competitors in consideration sets.

The old linear funnel, with marketing measured on leads and sales on revenue, is obsolete. A modern commercial strategy integrates all functions, operates against a shared revenue target, and uses stage-by-stage indicators only as diagnostics to improve the system. The measure of success is singular: did the strategy capture the revenue opportunity in the defined time? If not, the indicators will reveal areas for improvement in execution, but they will not redefine success.

CHAPTER 8

Preparing, Executing, Measuring, & Optimizing

Synopsis

Modern commercial success requires more than simply adopting the newest tools. Technology has given commercial teams extraordinary capabilities for targeting, personalization, and measurement. But too often these tools tempt teams to abide by their processes without a coherent commercial strategy, leaving much of their potential unrealized. Technology should not dictate the strategy; it should support and extend it. When aligned with insight and purpose, tools amplify effectiveness and accelerate results.

At the same time, the industry has become obsessed with measurement. Every click, view, and form fill is tracked, yet such fixation on metrics often distracts teams from the real objective: moving technical buyers toward adoption and driving revenue. The challenge is not in the data themselves but in how companies allow them to shape decisions, often at the expense of strategic thinking and market-shaping execution. In a rapidly changing landscape, the biggest risk isn't taking a chance on an unmeasurable strategy; it's continuing to do what everyone else is doing and expecting different results.

In this chapter, we will discuss:

- How to put technology in service of a strong commercial strategy
- The cost of the obsession with measurement
- Practical ways to balance speed, accuracy, and impact in execution
- How to identify and measure what truly matters for long-term commercial success

Let us explore a modern approach that drives actual, meaningful change.

Technology as an Enabler, Not a Strategy

Technology is one of the most powerful assets available to commercial teams. The ability to track buyer behavior across touchpoints, personalize experiences in real time, and deliver messaging at scale has transformed how companies reach and engage technical buyers. These capabilities, once unimaginable, now sit in the hands of almost every commercial team.

The mistake is assuming that having the tool equals having a strategy or employing innovation equals being innovative. Installing a CRM system does not create a customer experience. Deploying an automation platform does not, on its own, nurture trust. Even AI, which can aggregate vast pools of patterns and maybe even achieve insights, cannot decide which insights matter most or how to use them to shape a market.

To be clear, employing technology is crucial to ensure commercial success. Technology magnifies strategy. If the strategy is weak, the technology will dilute the brand, accelerating failure. If the strategy is strong, technology becomes an engine that extends its reach and precision. Commercial leaders must therefore approach tools as enablers, not as substitutes for strategic thinking.

Moving Beyond Measurement Obsession

The phrase "If you can't measure it, it's not important," though well-intentioned, has quietly distorted how commercial teams operate. It has created a culture where measurability itself becomes the goal, even if the metric being measured has little connection to commercial success.

This is how initiatives that have the potential to reshape perception, build preference, or deepen trust are sidelined because they don't produce a neat column in a dashboard. One commercial leader once rejected a bold brand awareness strategy with the words: "This program doesn't generate leads. My performance is measured on lead generation, so I can't support this." Had it been executed, the initiative would have positioned the company as a thought leader in a critical therapeutic area. Instead, it was abandoned in favor of another lead generation campaign, producing numbers instead of results.

This fixation on metrics produces three negative effects:

1. **It stifles innovation.** Teams avoid bold strategies in favor of tactics that are easily tracked.
2. **It fragments focus.** Sales and marketing teams argue over the quality of "leads" instead of collaborating around the buyer's actual journey.
3. **It rewards the wrong behaviors.** Success becomes defined by volume of activity rather than commercial impact.

The irony is that most commercial professionals already know this. When I speak with commercial leaders, they recognize that their audience rarely buy in linear paths. They see that a webinar attendee may ignore three follow-up emails, only to resurface months later with a purchase order. They know that preference, credibility, and authority often matter more than clicks. Yet systems of measurement, and the incentives tied to them, keep pushing their teams back toward narrow, transactional metrics.

The alternative is not to abandon measurement but to reframe it. Metrics should inform strategy, not define it. The right question has never been "What can we measure?" but instead it's "What signals tell us if we are shaping the market, building trust, and moving buyers toward adoption?"

When leveraged as intended, data become a tool for diagnosis and adjustment, rather than a cage that restricts action. Executing on an Insights-Led Model for Commercial Strategy that follows the buying journey of technical professionals, each data point can inform the exact position that technical buyers occupy in their journey and what to do next.

Expedience: Getting it Done Fast, or Getting it Done Smart

Execution in commercial strategy often balances between two extreme circumstances: the deadline-driven initiative (i.e., countless product launches at an upcoming tradeshow or conference) and the perfection-driven initiative (i.e., multiple rounds of message testing, creative tweaking, and A/B schemes). Both are costly.

Speed matters because markets move fast. Competitors launch, buyers shift, and technologies evolve. A delayed strategy may be a market loss. But speed must not come at the expense of coherence. Commercial initiatives rushed to market without alignment across sales and marketing teams may create noise, but rarely deliver impact.

On the other hand, companies sometimes overinvest in polishing. Many hours are spent debating minor design elements, testing messages that have strayed so far from the strategy in service of creative excellence, or optimizing for clicks that have little to no bearing on outcomes. This is also sometimes a byproduct of large teams without clear decision rights. Feedback from a large group typically results in significant dilution of the initiative's strategic potential. I have never experienced a feedback session from a large group actually improve a campaign's potential. All of this consumes resources and delays deployment, while potential buyers continue making decisions without the benefit of the company's perspective.

The solution lies in a disciplined process. Teams should assign clear decision rights: who approves strategic alignment, who validates technical accuracy, who signs off on creative, who architects all of the channels, and who sells. By clarifying roles and limiting revisions or strategic drift toward mediocrity, initiatives can move quickly while maintaining integrity.

While decision authority is commonly clear within the sales organization, I often encounter a misalignment between accountability and authority, especially in marketing. Frequently, marketing leaders are given the accountability to deliver on an initiative, but not the authority to make final decisions, needing to solicit input or approval from stakeholders unqualified in commercial expertise. Those with true expertise in marketing and commercial excellence should have the final say, and that is typically the most senior marketing executive. There needs to be clear communications and boundaries for authority before accountabilities can be bestowed and accepted.

A disciplined approach to internal decision-making reduces wasted cycles, protects the strategy's accuracy, and most importantly, keeps the focus on delivering value to the market rather than satisfying internal preferences.

Accuracy: Getting it Done Well

If speed ensures relevance, accuracy ensures credibility. In commercial strategy, accuracy is multi-dimensional:

- **Strategic accuracy:** Every document, touchpoint and asset must reinforce the broader positioning and value proposition.
- **Experiential accuracy:** Messaging through every channel must be consistent with brand tone, visual identity, texture, and the expectations of technical professionals.
- **Information accuracy:** Claims, data, references, case studies and testimonials must be verifiable and precise.

Failure in any of these areas undermines credibility. Technical buyers, in particular, are unforgiving when confronted with shallow data or overstated claims. Once trust is lost, it is rarely regained.

The best way to safeguard accuracy is to build checks into the process early. Reviewing messaging before starting design avoids expensive rework later. Aligning stakeholders early prevents "last-minute" objections or strategic drift that derail campaigns. And documenting accuracy sign-offs ensures accountability while reducing unnecessary second-guessing.

Ultimately, accuracy is about respect: respect for the buyer's intelligence, respect for the brand's credibility, and respect for the team's time.

Measuring What Matters

The final step is measurement, but measurement with purpose. Every commercial strategy must ultimately be judged against one metric: revenue within the reasonably allocated timeline. Did the strategy enable the company to capture its fair share of the market? If the answer is yes, then the strategy worked, regardless of how many leads were generated along the way.

Other metrics serve as **indicators**, not as goals. They can signal whether Leadership messaging is gaining attention, whether Education messaging is driving understanding, or whether Persuasion messaging is building confidence. But they should never replace revenue as the ultimate measure of success.

When measurement is aligned to strategy, commercial teams ask different kinds of questions:

- Are we shaping perception in our category?
- Are technical buyers engaging in ways that reflect trust and curiosity?
- Are our combined sales and marketing efforts creating conditions that reduce risk and reinforce adoption for prospective customers?

The answers to these questions are indicators that predict long-term success. Rarely answered through direct readouts of performance metrics, these questions are sometimes harder to quantify. Dashboards alone cannot answer them; they require judgment, context, and a willingness to look beyond the spreadsheet. However, they are closer to the truth of commercial impact.

Closing Thoughts

Technology has expanded what commercial teams can achieve, but its value is realized only when placed in service of a strong strategy. Metrics can guide execution, but they cannot replace critical thinking or vision. The companies that thrive use technology to amplify insight, measure what truly matters, and stay focused on the only metric that defines commercial success: revenue.

The danger of our current era is not a lack of tools or data. It is the temptation to let those tools and data dictate decisions, rather than to use them as instruments of a bold, insights-led commercial strategy.

The future belongs to companies willing to reclaim that balance: those brave enough to prioritize strategy, courageous enough to innovate beyond what is measurable, disciplined enough to execute with both speed and accuracy, and visionary enough to innovate the commercial function altogether.

CHAPTER 9

Innovation as a Commercial Imperative

Synopsis

I am on a mission to bring innovation into sales and marketing within healthcare and life science. Three decades of experience in commercial strategy across healthcare and life science has taught me that innovation comes from curiosity, insight, and the courage to challenge assumptions about how audiences think and act.

Innovation is not optional for commercial teams. It is as much a mandate for sales and marketing as it is for R&D or product development. Without innovation, organizations stagnate, competitors seize the advantage, and commercial professionals lose the ability to shape markets.

In this chapter, I will make the case for:

- The common cultural and structural reasons why commercial innovation stalls
- The eight types of innovation and the adoption lifecycle

- Practical tools for systematically generating innovative ideas
- Why innovation must become part of commercial mindset and culture

Where Should Innovation Come From?

When I first left my career as a biochemist in the mid-1990s, the internet was a novelty. The majority of the companies I worked with didn't have a website, and some pushed back against this new technology.

"A website? Being on the internet is beyond the scope of this company!" the head of sales and marketing from an independent fume hood manufacturer once scoffed at me.

It's laughable now, yet it illustrates a recurring pattern: companies resist change until it is no longer optional. Print advertising gave way to banner ads, native advertising, and account-based marketing. Sales people dropping off printed brochures evolved to sophisticated personalized communications. Direct mail gave way to email and later to social media.

Each shift was hailed as "innovation." But that's wrong.

These shifts demonstrate teams who adopted tools, but adoption is not innovation. True innovation requires the willingness to rethink how commercial teams engage with their buyers. Without it, sales and marketing risk becoming forgettable. And as hyper-competition looms, being forgettable is fatal.

In healthcare and life science, innovation is not limited to the R&D or product development groups. Healthcare organizations often experience innovation originating from commercial teams, but that's not nearly as common in technical life science companies. In healthcare companies, brand teams often work hand in hand with insights and analytics groups to truly understand their market and sense behavior shifts, and then develop innovation territories based on cultural and industry trends. They hear frustrations firsthand. They observe needs their markets don't even realize they have. They notice the subtle behaviors that product-centric teams may otherwise miss. This perspective, when paired with the right tools, can become the spark for breakthroughs that change the trajectory of entire markets.

Why Commercial Teams Don't Apply Innovation

The reasons for a lack of innovation within the commercial organization are rarely about individual effort or creativity. Most commercial professionals are deeply committed to serving customers and eager to find new ways forward. The challenge lies in the systems and incentives within the organization.

1. Structural dependence on tools

Upon adoption of a technology, many organizations have normalized processes and have created the roles as dictated by their tech stacks. This significantly reduces the commercial organization's ability to develop ideas outside of their tool-directed processes, crippling organizations from applying creativity to their commercial challenges.

2. Metric fixation

To further narrow the possibilities, team members' performances are equated with marketing metrics (i.e., lead generation). Company culture is optimized for the wrong outcome and the collective mindset of the commercial team runs the significant risk of missing big gold mines in favor of small wins. This sometimes becomes akin to collecting pennies among a mountain of gold.

3. An intolerance for experimentation

Innovation requires experimentation and can represent risk. Many commercial teams often operate in do-or-die situations (I'm exaggerating, but when the product is late to market, deadlines loom, and stakeholders expect significant revenue growth every 90 days, it certainly feels this way), and there is simply no room for risk. Pragmatic commercial teams keep employing the tactics they know in favor of predictability, regardless of impact. Ironically, few commercial teams calculate the risk of failure due to risk-aversion.

Any combination of these three dynamics means that innovation suffocates. Commercial teams lose any incentive to think creatively about buyer behavior, and they default to playing defense.

Commercial strategy is a game that is won by strong offense. And embracing innovation is a mandate.

The Eight Types of Innovation

Purposeful innovation requires a re-examination of the technology adoption life cycle. Most healthcare and life science companies want to extend the relevance of their products and services to as many potential customers as possible. Different types of innovation enable maximum market adoption.

In the book *Dealing with Darwin*, Geoffrey Moore introduced eight types of innovation that provide a framework for expanding how sales and marketing teams should consider as a market matures. Figure 9-1, maps each innovation to the phases of Moore's technology adoption lifecycle, and descriptions of each type of innovation follow.

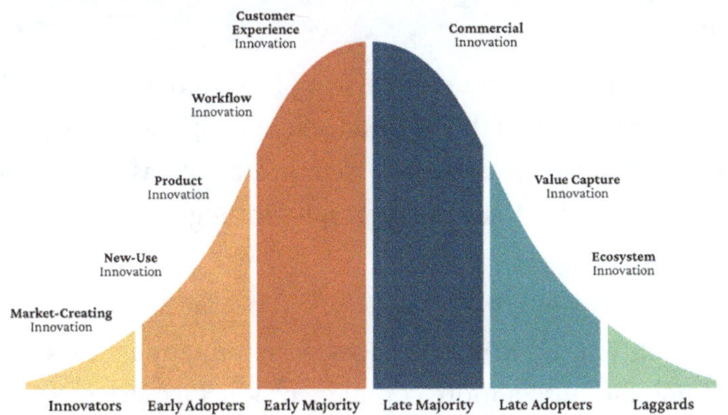

Figure 9-1. Types of innovation across the technology adoption lifecycle. Different types of innovation are most effective at different stages of the technology adoption lifecycle, from disruptive innovators to late adopters. (Concept inspired by and adapted from Geoffrey Moore book, Dealing with Darwin: How Great Companies Innovate at Every Phase of their Innovation).

The following takes Geoffrey Moore's framework and adapts it to healthcare and life science.

Market-Creating Innovation

This type of innovation creates entirely new markets or completely reshapes existing ones. Uber did this by transforming urban transportation; in life science, direct-to-consumer genetic testing was a disruptive play. Market-creating innovation is clearly risky because it requires commercial teams to inspire customers out of their routines and convinces them to go through a painful and disruptive process of significant change. But when it succeeds, it redefines entire industries.

New-Use Innovation

New-use innovation takes existing technologies and finds specific, new uses for them. Next Generation DNA Sequencing (NGS) was developed as a research tool, but it has now found significant applicability in diagnostics through liquid biopsy.

Product Innovation

Product innovation combines or advances existing technologies into a more complete product experience. The iPhone is a prime example of product innovation. At the time, cell phones, digital cameras, digital assistants, and digital music players were all in early adoption stages, but Apple unified them into a single device. This integration accelerated adoption across multiple categories and redefined customer expectations.

Workflow Innovation

Creating a new process or workflow to procure or use an offering can unlock new groups of customers. Grocery delivery is an example of workflow innovation, where the end goal is still obtaining ingredients and nourishment, but ordered and received in a novel way. In healthcare and life sciences, vending machine-style "supply/freezer programs" enable technical professionals to instantly access the most common consumables they need.

Customer Experience Innovation

This type of innovation transforms how people interact with an offering. The offering stays the same, while customers' experience of it changes. The fitness company Peloton demonstrated experiential innovation by bringing the cycling classroom to the home. Another powerful example of customer experience innovation is the "Hospital at Home" at Tampa General Hospital's program, where patients receive hospital-level care in their own homes. As of this writing, this program has proven to improve patient outcomes with dramatically reduced readmission rates.

Commercial Innovation

Commercial innovation involves creating new ways to engage with customers. Quartzy, a distributor of scientific chemicals, reagents, and other consumables created a new marketing channel by providing a free lab inventory management app to its audiences. As scientists manage the inventory of their consumables in the lab, they are given the opportunity to make a purchase of low-inventory or expiring material, directly from their app. This not only circumvents a very noisy media landscape, but it also invokes a sense of reciprocity with its audiences. As a result, Quartzy is able to deliver a far more personalized experience.

Value Capture Innovation

This type of innovation requires changing how a company makes money or delivers value, often through a novel business model. As one of the largest suppliers of laboratory products, equipment, reagents and consumables, Thermo Fisher Scientific expanded from capturing value through sales of its products to also capturing value by offering contract research, development, and manufacturing services.

Ecosystem Innovation

Reshaping the framework of an industry by redefining relationships, roles, and flows of value across the ecosystem, this type of innovation reorganizes the system itself. Imagine a venture capital firm that provides significant shared services, including lab space, the latest scientific equipment and fractional business leaders, and creates a marketplace of potential buyers or next-phase investors for the most promising technologies arising as a result of the innovation of its many biotech firms. The venture capital firm Curie.bio is creating this exact ecosystem. By significantly consolidating the otherwise-disparate actors along the value chain, the firm can enjoy potentially higher returns for its investors.

When mapped against the technology adoption life cycle, it is clear where commercial teams need to apply innovation to generate value for the company.

Knowing which type of innovation to pursue is only half the battle. The other half is systemically generating innovative ideas that align with the company's commercial strategy and fostering a culture of daily innovation within the marketing and sales teams.

Tools for Bringing Innovation Back

A highly seasoned product leader once told me that the sales of his product line were slowly declining, and he believed the entire product category was becoming commodified. When I suggested we perform ethnographic, or qualitative, research to observe customers' behaviors, he said, "I'm not going to learn anything useful by watching a bunch of scientists pipette all day. I came from the lab. I know what their work entails." This is exactly the wrong stance to take when innovation is desperately needed, as was this product manager's case.

Three tools are particularly effective at reigniting innovative thinking: **qualitative research, ethnography** and **scenario building**.

Qualitative Research

The opportunity for innovation often hides in plain sight. It comes from curiosity, patience, and the willingness to see the world as customers see it. As I have covered earlier in this book, qualitative research methodologies are terrific for identifying these opportunities.

If implemented correctly, they force managers to abandon orthodoxies and consider the world from a fresh perspective. Qualitative research methods can be implemented through:

- Advisory boards
- Focus groups
- In-depth interviews
- Ethnographic studies

While most sales and marketing teams are familiar with qualitative research techniques, they find it difficult to go beneath the surface to understand the respondents' true, human-level motivations for their behavior. Instead they hold scientific or clinical discussions, mapping a rational understanding of changes, but never achieving the repeatable triggers that would inform how they can solicit the desired response and action from their audience. On the other hand, trained behavioral researchers can guide conversations to identify real behavioral triggers by exploring the central tensions that dictate buyers' choices and then exploring how those tensions drive technical professionals to act.

Ethnography

One of the most powerful techniques for innovation is conducting ethnographic research. Ethnography means observing how technical professionals actually behave, not just what they say. By entering their workplace for full sensory immersion, watching workflows, looking for frustrations displayed by body language, noticing small inefficiencies, and observing habits formed to overcome those inefficiencies, commercial teams can uncover insights that surveys miss.

By engaging in the world of the target audience, not as an expert or peer, but as an observant with beginner's eyes, commercial teams can see what others miss, because they are too busy engaging on a different level with their customers.

Scenario Building

While traditional forecasting and planning processes are rooted in ample data and many market dynamics are factored into their consensus estimates, they usually paint a singular vision of the future with very little tolerance for deviation from the singular prediction.

Business leaders want confidence to make the right decisions, which is why they desire predictions of the future. Instead of predicting a single future, leaders will be more successful if they prepare for a range of possible futures and sense ahead of their competition which future is unfolding.

Scenario building is a rigorous exercise that assumes the future is plural and uncertain. By mapping critical and uncertain forces such as political, technological, cultural, scientific, and environmental, commercial teams create a range of plausible futures.

At LINUS, this technique allowed us to anticipate how the disruption of COVID-19 would affect scientific productivity. We examined the interplay of global interdependence and potential supply chain shocks. No one predicted the pandemic or how it would affect the life science industry. But we had a scenario for how it was likely to play out. How did we do this? **We identified the driving forces and asked, "How is X, which may not actually be connected to Y, going to affect us?"** We used scenario planning to map out exactly what was going to happen to productivity in the life sciences. We created graphs and webinars talking about the four phases leading to the scenario that ultimately became the global pandemic.

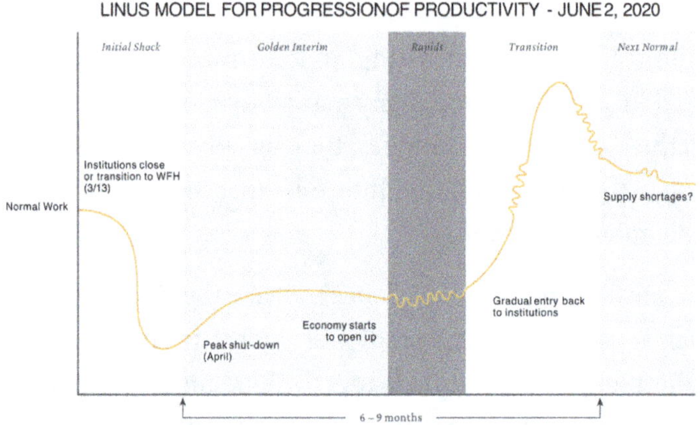

Figure 9-2: *The LINUS model for progression of productivity, June 2020.*

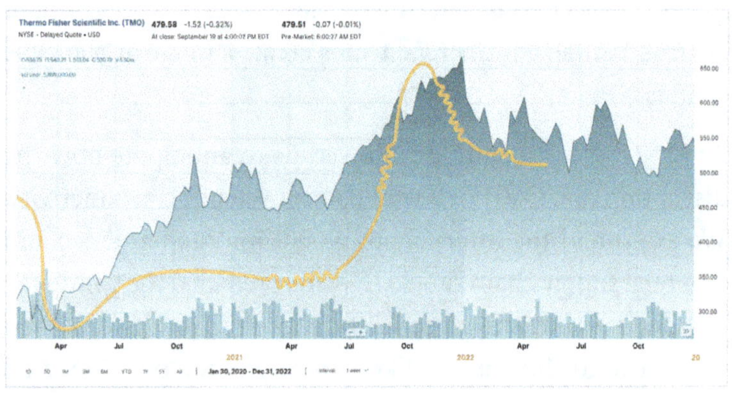

Figure 9-3: *The LINUS model for how scientific productivity would be affected due to disruptions resulting from the COVID-19 pandemic correctly predicted the overall progression as well as some*

of the derivative effects such as supply shocks. It did not correctly predict timing. For reference, compare the rough shape of the LINUS model with the actual stock performance of Thermo Fisher Scientific, a broad, global provider of scientific tools and services.

Scenario building frees teams from rigid plans and gives them resilience. It encourages bold thinking, hard choices, and agility in the face of change. But merely performing the act of scenario planning can provide commercial teams with a sandbox for innovation.

When building your scenarios, score each driving force for how *critical* they are and how *uncertain* it is in the timeframe that you are using to build your scenarios. Then, take the two most critical and uncertain, and map them against each other. That's how you begin telling four separate stories that emerge at the intersection of these two critical uncertainties.

What would the world look like if there was a ridiculous amount of economic growth but scientific progress declined, for example? Or vice versa? Instead of asking why they matter, you tell the story of these worlds to create scenarios. Now, you are in a better position to prepare for the future. You have to make hard decisions and be prepared to pivot. This is how you create innovative thinking—by creating plausible scenarios and discussing the implications for your business.

Final Thoughts on Innovation

Innovation is not optional. It is a mandate for every function within your organization, including sales and marketing. When commercial teams confuse technology adoption with innovation or allow measurement fixation to paralyze them, they miss the opportunity to shape an industry or a market.

But when they embrace curiosity, apply the eight types of innovation, and practice using tools like ethnography and scenario planning, they generate insights that cannot be copied. They create conditions where change is not feared but welcomed, where risk is managed intelligently, and where competitive advantage is renewed again and again.

Companies thrive not when commercial teams wait for innovation to arrive from the lab, but when they take ownership of it themselves. The Insights-Led Model for Commercial Strategy is designed to increase the incidence of innovative ideas.

CHAPTER 10

What to Do When the Internal Team is Not Buying It

Synopsis

Let us address one of the hardest truths of commercial strategy: even the most powerful frameworks and innovative ideas will stall in the face of organizational resistance to change. Implementing new ways of working requires courage, cultural alignment, and clarity in execution.

Change is never easy, but it is possible. Whether you are the CEO of a global enterprise, a manager responsible for a team, or an individual contributor, and whether you started your career journey before the internet was a novelty or have never experienced a workplace that doesn't leverage AI, you have the ability to shape how change happens. This chapter shows you:

- Why challenges must be faced directly

- Practical strategies for creating cultural and organizational shifts
- The enduring importance of critical thinking in a tech-obsessed world

My goal is simple: to leave you not only with tools, but with confidence that meaningful change is within reach.

Culture Eats Strategy for Breakfast

The trope "culture eats strategy for breakfast" isn't a dismissal of strategy, but rather a reminder that no strategy can thrive without acknowledging the culture it must live within. Too often, commercial strategies are developed with so much focus on the market or the competition that little thought is given to whether the organization is capable of supporting them. Even the most potent strategy will struggle if it demands behaviors or norms the company is not willing to adopt.

For example, a company led by scientists who thrive in the world of invention cannot be expected to suddenly transform into a people-centric culture. That does not mean such an organization is incapable of commercial excellence. It does mean that the strategy must build on the organization's natural strengths while thoughtfully addressing its gaps. The role of brand strategy is to celebrate the most noble aspects of the actual internal culture, otherwise the public will see right through the attempt to be something the company's culture doesn't actually represent.

Every commercial strategy needs a "cultural appendix" which catalogs an honest look at how the organization must adapt to enable success. If the company is risk-averse, the strategy must acknowledge that innovation will require more evidence, proof points, and internal persuasion before ideas are greenlit. If the leadership team is hierarchical, execution plans should build in clear lines of authority and decision rights rather than assuming a flat, collaborative structure that doesn't exist.

Cultural alignment is not about developing excuses for suboptimal performance. It is about sequencing internal change so that a strategy has the support system it needs to thrive. Leaders must ask: What will our organization need to believe, feel, and practice differently for this strategy to work? Only when that question is answered can a strategy move from theory to impact. And if change is necessary, leaders must face the challenge head-on.

Facing Change Head-On

Change feels threatening to organizations because it interrupts routines, relationships, predictable outcomes, and comfort zones. People resist change not because of laziness or lack of intelligence or motivation, but because it is human nature to avoid discomfort. And change is uncomfortable. However, leaders can make a difference by creating experiences that help teams move forward together. **The key to orchestrating change is to instigate a new experience for team members before they realize they are changing their behavior.**

Consider a scenario I witnessed at a company where two senior leaders were locked in conflict. After months of interventions, teams felt divided and caught in an energetic vortex while productivity plummeted. The CEO made the difficult decision to part ways with one of the leaders; someone who was beloved by the rest of the team. Morale dropped, trust eroded, and productivity became an afterthought.

Rather than glossing over the tension or waiting it out, the CEO walked directly into it. She acknowledged the loss, invited honest dialogue, and then did something bold: she asked the remaining employees to co-develop the company's strategy during an offsite retreat held entirely outdoors without the typical presentation decks, whiteboards, or markers.

During the first few hours, employees remained guarded, avoiding eye contact and engaging only with suspicion. By the retreat's end, however, these same employees were buzzing with energy. They had inadvertently authored a new company culture and experienced it firsthand. Months later, the transformation remained palpable: productivity was higher, communication was better, and a sense of camaraderie permeated every interaction.

Engineering Experiences That Drive Change

While many assume people must first change their beliefs to change behavior, in practice, the reverse is often true. As the above example illustrates, experiences can reshape beliefs. By creating experiences that model the desired feelings, barriers to change are lowered.

Change cannot be commanded into existence. Edicts from leaders, often delivered through company-wide emails announcing a "new culture" usually do not affect any change.

What works is engineering experiences that make the change tangible and felt over and over again

Another client faced a very different challenge: employees were disengaged and productivity lagged. The environment, a sea of cubicles under harsh fluorescent lights, embodied monotony. A new, ambitious Chief Commercial Officer wanted to change the culture of the organization. But he didn't start with speeches. He started by moving the furniture.

By shifting cubicles 45 degrees and creating a central open area with couches and whiteboards, he disrupted the norm, forcing new experiences and new interaction. As employees needed to walk through the central area on the way to a conference room, the kitchen or bathroom, conversations began. Ideas flowed. Funny drawings appeared on white boards. Pranks were pulled. Collaboration rekindled. Productivity rebounded.

To achieve big change, leaders can start with small change, and this initial step can be anything, so long as it transmits the feeling that something is different about this interaction.

The Modern Workplace

Modern commercial teams are increasingly remote, and this adds another layer of complexity. With employees scattered across geographies and time zones, culture can feel diluted or invisible. Virtual communications tools that every business relies on often lack the connection necessary for transformation.

This does not make change impossible, but it requires more creativity. Leaders must design intentional moments of togetherness. A virtual happy hour cannot replicate an immersive experience, but a thoughtfully planned offsite can. Even the architecture of an event can send signals: a narrow hallway creates scarcity, a platform confers authority, a welcoming entrance invites inclusion.

These subtle meta communications speak volumes, and it's important to carefully engineer such experiences. People naturally crave togetherness, and remote work does not eliminate this need. Remote work keeps teams apart, but it hasn't erased the human need for belonging. Leaders who create opportunities for meaningful connection will overcome resistance more effectively than those who solely rely on communication tools and platitudes.

Achieving Execution Excellence

Effective execution of commercial programs requires a cohesively functional organization across all departments within the company. This brings organizational dynamics into consideration. Execution excellence is less about heroic individual performance and more about creating the conditions in which every team member can act with clarity and confidence.

In a landmark *Harvard Business Review* study titled *The Secrets to Successful Strategy Execution*, Gary Neilson, Karla Martin, and Elizabeth Powers analyzed thousands of responses across multiple industries to assess their companies' abilities to execute. The study determined four principal drivers of execution excellence: **information flow, decision rights, motivators, and organizational structure.** The authors found that the first two were twice as effective in driving execution excellence as the last two. Yet many companies devote disproportionate energy to tweaking the less effective levers, developing bonus programs, comp plans, and constant reorganization. Let us actually examine the two less-common, but more effective principal drivers.

Information Flow: The Fuel for Execution

When each team member understands the direction the organization is moving and how their personal efforts contribute to progress, they become more effective. This can only be achieved in organizations with proper, systematic information flow.

Smaller teams are naturally more conducive to proper information flow due to proximity of team members, but overreliance on proximity masks the lack of systematic information flow, limiting the team's growth potential. As small companies attempt to scale, silos form, creating formal barriers for information, and information flow becomes constricted by meetings or often poorly adopted technologies.

Communication requires discipline, transparency, and intentional processes. For commercial teams, this means sharing the development process of strategies instead of sudden reveals of fully formed plans, followed by death-by-slides style "training."

Having seen too many brilliant strategies fail to reach their potential, my team at LINUS always develops an internal communications strategy as standard practice for all of our engagements with a goal to actively engage the entire team (or even the entire company) through every stage of development. By the time the strategy is fully developed and approved, we experience a more engaged internal team who is both intellectually and emotionally committed to realizing the strategy or plan.

Decision Rights: Where Accountability Meets Authority

Often conflated with "roles and responsibilities," decision rights are the specific boundaries that define the choices an individual can make without being questioned or seeking approval.

Team members need to be trusted to do their jobs, yet well-intentioned processes often result in misaligned decision rights. A marketer told to generate demand but needing sign-off at every creative step or a salesperson tasked with reducing close times but bound by cumbersome approval chains, is held accountable for goals but doesn't have the proper authority to ensure they are met. These situations are common causes of friction among commercial teams.

True execution excellence comes when accountability and authority align. Every team member should be able to answer three questions unambiguously: What is in my remit? What is the business counting on me to deliver? What are the consequences to the business if I succeed or fail? Leaders are also responsible for negotiating decision rights in team collaborations.

Focusing on What Matters

Execution excellence emerges not from constant restructuring or superficial incentives, but from ensuring that information flows freely, decision rights are unambiguous, and people are trusted to do the jobs they were hired to do. Commercial teams that get these fundamentals right create the conditions in which strategy can thrive, even in complex and distributed organizations.

Continuing the Conversation

The strategies in this book are timeless and adaptable. I've spent three decades helping commercial teams and organizations transform their marketing and sales approaches and although much has changed, these concepts have remained the same.

If you're interested in bringing these ideas to your team or organization through a keynote presentation or workshop, you can learn more about my speaking topics and approach at **thelinusgroup.com/speaking.**

Conclusion

As an audience, scientists, doctors, engineers and even CFOs are professional skeptics, and they will only continue to sharpen their ability to ignore efforts to capture their attention and a share of their wallet. They are just not buying it.

Committing to the Insights-Led Model for Commercial Strategy does not require any organizational restructure or necessitate massive technology infrastructure investments. It does require a focus on technical professionals as people, the bravery to be imaginative, and the dedication to develop and execute meaningful, worthwhile strategies for audiences through their technical buying journey.

Until the day when marketing is no longer seen as mere coordination and instead becomes the center stage of corporate strategy, and salespeople are no longer seen as order-takers but market makers, commercial teams must strive to demonstrate value within the organizational culture. The only path is to deliver a true and measurable force multiplier to the products, services, and companies that hold the promise of improving human lives and the collective health of our planet. This book has been about filling gaps in current healthcare and life science practices and formalizing strategy development and execution to fulfill its great potential.

There is no shortage of commercial know-how in our industries. Many brilliant minds have ample formal training in the technical aspects of science, medicine, business administration, or all of the above. As our industries have reached new heights, it is time to formalize and unify commercial practices, so companies can seize even larger opportunities. Systematically adopting the practices outlined in this book, boldly challenging the status quo, and relentlessly innovating carry the potential to transform the perceived value of the discipline of the commercial function within our industry.

In December 2021, as Dr. Francis Collins was retiring from his role as the director of the National Institutes of Health (NIH), he was asked in an interview what he wished the NIH could have done differently during the pandemic. He lamented, "Boy, there are things about human behavior that I don't think we had invested enough into understanding."[2]

I have dedicated my career to making sure we never suffer from such oversight again.

I hope that by applying the content in this book, innovative commercial teams in healthcare and life science will be energized and deliver revolutionary results. The pathway I have outlined in these pages is the best way I know how to do it. I have seen it succeed. I eagerly await the magic that you will put into it and add to it to take it to the next level.

---

2   Selena Simmons-Duffin, "The NIH Director on Why Americans Aren't Getting Healthier, despite Medical Advances," NPR, December 7, 2021, https://www.npr.org/sections/health-shots/2021/12/07/1061940326/the-nih-director-on-why-americans-arent-getting-healthier-despite-medical-advanc.

Acknowledgements

This book is a celebration of all of the people that I have been lucky to learn from, who have generously shared with me their time, wisdom, patience and friendship.

I'm grateful for the hundreds of people who have spent part of their career journey at LINUS. You are brilliant, passionate, and creative, and it has been my honor to serve you and to watch you grow. I have also been humbled by all of your grace and patience as you have inspired me to grow. You teach me so much about strategy, leadership and being a better person. Throughout the decades, so many of you have become the captains of industry at some of the leading brands in the world. I'm especially thankful for my business partner, Kristin Apple, whose vision transformed LINUS into an innovation powerhouse and has made our time together feel like a fun, amazing adventure.

The professionals in our industry who pour their hearts and souls in pushing the boundaries of science and healthcare continue to inspire me, especially those with whom we have had the privilege to collaborate. Everything I have learned in my career has been the result of collaborations. I thank all of our clients who share with us some of their toughest commercialization challenges, giving us the opportunity to advance our thinking and to further their success.

Many mentors have shown me the way and have been patient with me through all of the growing up that I have had to do. To name every person would fill more pages than this entire book. I am especially thankful for executives who have spent time with me through the years, teaching me about different facets of business and strategy. I thank Dara Grantham Wright, Lisa Sellers, Kenneth Yoon, Peter Fromen, Thierry Bernard, Christian Henry, Sam Raha, David Weber, Jasmine Gruia-Gray, Katherine Andersen, Delphine Caraguel, Suzanne Graham, Amy Butler, Hrissi Samartzidou, Andy Bertera, Emily LeProust, Paddy Finn, Peter Siesel, Luke Timmerman, Ted Love, and Giovanna Prout. I hold all of your continued success dearly in my heart.

A special thanks to Gina Mullane, Kristen Eisenhauer, Jim Foster, and the team at Charles River Laboratories, not only for an opportunity of a lifetime to push the boundaries by creating the campaign chronicled in this book, but also for permission to tell the story of our journey together.

To call Mark O'Brien a colleague or a friend would leave so much out of the picture. Mark has been both, and so much more. I am inspired by Mark and his entire team at Newfangled, for their mastery in the work they do and for the culture they have built.

Of course, life is so much more than work, and without friends and family it would feel one dimensional. I owe so much to my dear friends David Haugaard and Brian Transeau, who have walked with me through dark and light.

In every attempt to acknowledge and thank my wife, Rebecca, words fail. I am deeply thankful to her for so much and for sharing this entire journey with me. Every day, every night, and with every breath in between, I am thankful for Ada.

Finally, I honor and celebrate the life of my dear mother, Marzieh, who gave me life in every sense of the word, who sacrificed so much to provide my brother and I with every opportunity to better ourselves, and who supported us with all of her might. Her last words to me will always bring tears of gratitude, as she whispered "I love you 'till the end of time." May she rest in peace.

About the Author

Hamid Ghanadan always wanted to find a third way. Being strongly encouraged by his family to study medicine or engineering, he found a third way to study both art and science. Exploring his job options, he was again encouraged by his advisors to choose between a career as a biochemist either in academia or in industry. Instead, Hamid founded the strategy firm—LINUS—in 1996, dedicating his career to studying human behavior within technical environments, and developing new models for marketing, strategic communications, future visioning and strategic planning. This path has offered Hamid many opportunities to find a third way: he is the author of two other books: Persuading Scientists and Catalytic Experiences. He is a frequent speaker at many industry events as well as the global stage at TEDx, and he is proud to have won several honors, including the SAMPS Lifetime Achievement Award and MM+M's Pinnacle award. He lives in Colorado with his family, helping his team and his clients to grow by finding a third way.

www.ingramcontent.com/pod-product-compliance
Lightning Source LLC
Chambersburg PA
CBHW071307030726
47594CB00002B/346